Memories are always
the best.
Terri J Dinkel

Oatmeal and Kisses

Terri Jeanne Tinkel

Copyright ©2011

by Terri Jeanne Tinkel

All rights reserved, including the right to reproduce this book, e-book, or portions thereof in any form whatsoever.

OATMEAL AND KISSES

*Oatmeal and kisses mean Mother to me
Both were a part of my childhood, you see.
Each morning at breakfast, there would be a big bowl
And Mother would say "Eat it −it'll keep out the cold."
Whenever the family was sick or got hurt
She'd kiss away the soreness and wash away the dirt.
Her kisses were tender and sweet on my face.
And I'd lovingly hug her as we shared an embrace.
Oatmeal and kisses the best part of my youth.
The best kind of medicine and that's God's sure enough truth.
Oh how I'd love to go backward in time
And share oatmeal and kisses with that mother of mine.
But she's up in heaven probably passing a bowl
And telling an angel, "It's good for your soul."*
　　　***

OATMEAL AND KISSES is written in memory of my mother and all my other female ancestors who contributed to the life I learned about, wrote about, and lived.

I love you all.

This book is based on poems and diaries and photographs that were saved and from stories I heard from some relatives. I did use my imagination for the dialog and tried to be true to what I believe might have happened.

Please forgive me if I was wrong....

And, of course, I did not intend to hurt anyone's feelings in writing this story.

PREFACE - JULY 1993...

They were all sitting in the new, freshly washed, very luxurious black limo thinking to themselves.

Then Suzanne spoke, "Damn, I just broke another fingernail."

Mary Margaret replied, "Well, I can see I will have to get a better manicure when I get home. There certainly aren't any experienced or even good licensed nail shops here."

Elizabeth thought, "Boy, if nothing else goes right, at least my nails always look great."

And Rachel said softly, "I wish I could let my nails grow but they just get in the way when I am working."

They started talking about memories and soon were laughing and sharing old stories. They could hardly control their giggles.

Finally Suzanne said, "Oh my goodness, we should be so ashamed. We're on our way to bury our mother and we're carrying on like this. I bet the limo driver for the funeral home thinks we are terrible!"

Suzanne's son, Gregg, who was sitting in the front passenger seat turned around and said, "I think Grandma would have loved this. You should write a book about her life...." **AND SO IT BEGAN.....**

CHAPTER ONE - 1932

Little Pattie Jean skipped down the street. She loved to go to the butcher shop to buy lunch meat for Mama. Even though she only had a few coins, she knew the butcher would give her a slice of any kind of lunch meat she wanted. She was always polite to him and spoke so sweetly. Her mother had told her a friendly smile and good manners made a big difference in the world.

Even though she was very shy, she thought "I'll ask for ham loaf this time. And next time, I'll ask for pickle pimento." She giggled to herself and smiled ever so slightly.

All of a sudden, she thought about the dream she sometimes had at night. In the dream, she was very, very small and she was talking to a little boy. They were talking about Mama! There was another boy there too but he was older and bigger than her. She felt like she knew them but she couldn't figure out who they were.

"I wonder why I keep having that silly dream." she whispered to herself.

Pattie Jean lived in an apartment in Chicago, IL. She was 8 years old and she had a sister and two little brothers. "I sure hope Mama doesn't

want me to take the boys to the park again today because she has another headache. Those boys never mind me and they get so dirty when they play outside. Then, Mama gets mad at me because they ruined their clothes."
      She sighed deeply. All Tommy and Mike did lately was argue and fight. They didn't really hurt each other but they sure tore up their clothes. Money wasn't very plentiful and Mama got really tired of doing the mending. She had never taken the time to teach Pattie Jean or her younger sister, Bettie, how to do housework, sew or even cook. Mama would rather have Pattie Jean take the children outside so she could have some peace. Usually she kept Bettie at home because Bettie was quiet and played by herself. And besides that, Bettie couldn't handle the boys. They made her cry when they wouldn't mind her.
      "Maybe if I walk slower, it will take me longer to get the lunch meat back home and it will be too late for the park today. I guess I could read them a story instead." Pattie Jean said to herself. "Oh, I could even make up a new story. They always like that".
      Poor Mama, she is always so sad when Papa isn't home. I wonder how long he will be gone this time.

CHAPTER TWO:

Pattie Jean knew her Mama loved her Papa very much. Papa tried so hard to bring home a little money every week. He was good at everything. He could fix things and built things and even make things that he thought about in his own head. He couldn't get a job that lasted more than a few weeks though because...sometimes he stayed at the tavern down the street too late at night.

Pattie Jean would hear Mama crying several times a week. She wished Papa would just stay home and play with them. He was so funny and he would play on the floor with the boys for hours; unless he went to that neighborhood tavern nearby. She especially loved it when Papa sang those old Irish songs too.

Pattie Jean was so proud of her Papa. He would make things for Mama out of scraps of wood sometimes. And most of the time they really worked! Some people were buying a covering for their kitchen floor called *lin-o-lee-um*. The pattern was pretty and you could wash it and it would stay shiny for a few days. And the best part was that you didn't get splinters from the old wood planks on the floor either.

Papa was trying to get a job putting this flcor cover down really fast for the customers. He had been working on a little knife thing to help him do it. He had a few jobs out of town and he would work on this knife at night. He said the faster he could get the job done, the more jobs he could get.

CHAPTER THREE:

One day Pattie Jean noticed that Mama didn't have on her little gold ring that she always wore on her "married" finger of her left hand. Pattie Jean looked all over the apartment for the ring but couldn't find it. Finally she asked Mama where it was.

Mama always said that Papa was a good man, but the *"spirits"* got him in trouble. Pattie Jean had never seen any ghosts around Papa but Mama sure did talk about those *"spirits"* when Papa didn't come right home. Mama wasn't scared of them ghosts but she sure got mad at them *"spirits."* She said they caused a whole lot of trouble for their family.

Mama worried about money all the time too. Mama told Pattie Jean that she had to pawn her ring for some money for food that week. All she had to cook was oatmeal and brown sugar. Pattie Jean remembered how delicious it tasted. Mama was such a good cook. She could make a lot of food out of very little. Even when there wasn't much food, there was always oatmeal. And there were plenty of hugs and kisses to go around.

CHAPTER FOUR:

A few weeks later, Mama said it was probably a good thing that they didn't have very many clothes or much furniture because this month they had to play a game called **"Get out of town."** The strange thing about this game was it was always played late at night and they had to move as quickly as possible when they played it. Mama would count and they had to be ready to go before she got to 500.

Usually Mama would wake them up in the middle of the night and they would all be as quiet as they could (except for those noisy boys) and tiptoe down the stairs past the landlord's apartment. They would take their clothes and whatever else they could carry and move to a new place by the next day. The best part of the game was they never knew where they would wind up living. It became a new adventure every few months.

It was fun to have a new neighborhood to live in. But sometimes when they played the game, it was cold and rainy or snowy. It was always dark and late at night. Pattie Jean would worry that Papa wouldn't find them. But he always did because Aunt Lucille could tell him where everyone had moved. If Papa was out of town for very long time, the moving game would be more often. But Papa always found them somehow.

   Pattie Jean liked to visit her Aunt Lucille. Aunt Lucille had a bigger apartment and pretty clothes and hats. She even had a telephone. Pattie Jean always watched carefully when Aunt Lucille used the telephone. She thought she could probably make a call all by herself, even though she had just had her birthday in January. Pattie Jean went over the whole thing in her head. First you have to take the little ear piece off the hook. Next you have to wind up the telephone several times with the 'winder" on the right side. When the **Op Rater** talks, you can ask her to find the person you want to talk to. Pattie Jean didn't know how the **Op Rater** did it but she almost always found the person and they came to talk on the Op Rater's very own telephone. It was so exciting! Almost better than getting free ice.   And that was an adventure in itself. Someday Pattie Jean wanted a telephone all for herself. She would even share the party line if the other people didn't talk on the phone too much. But, maybe that was why it was called a "party line" because you were supposed to have a party talking to everyone on the same phone line.

After one of their night time moves, Aunt Lucille called and told Mama about a photographer who wanted to take pictures of the little girls, Pattie Jean and Bettie. He said he would give the photograph to the store illustrator who drew the classified ads for the department store where Aunt Lucille worked. In return, the little girls could keep the dresses they wore and the doll they played with in the photograph. Aunt Lucille said she would take the girls to the store for the picture and bring them back home. The best part of all was that Mama got a photograph of her little girls along with 2 new dresses for them. And the doll, of course.

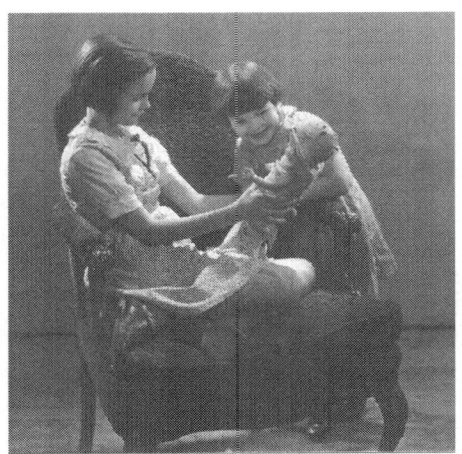

Pattie Jean and Bettie modeling. - 1936

CHAPTER FIVE:

After a few years, Papa came home with a pocket full of money. The family got to move to a bigger apt. They even moved during the day! Papa tried to get Mama's ring back from the pawn shop but they must have lost it because he said they couldn't find it anymore. It had been about 3 years since she pawned it.

Everyone got new clothes and new shoes. Mama cooked a big dinner and it wasn't even a holiday! Papa said he got a **PAT-TENT** for his knife invention. Pattie Jean didn't know what a **PAT-TENT** was but it must have been a very special camping tent because Papa was really excited about it. Pattie Jean thought it would be fun to sleep in the **PAT-TENT** overnight in the back yard but Papa didn't bring it home. However, he did talk to a man at Sears and Roebuck who hired him to work six days a week installing the *lin-o-lee-um* for their store. He used his knife invention and was able to complete jobs very quickly. Mama was real happy but she still worried about the tavern in the neighborhood. No matter where or how often they moved, Papa always found the tavern. And the *"spirits"* managed to find him too, regardless of where they moved.

CHAPTER SIX:

As the years went by, the family's living spaces got bigger. The family expanded again with the arrival of Billy and then Kathy. Now there were 6 children to clothe and feed and raise. Their names were Pattie Jean, Bettie, Michael, Thomas, William and Kathleen.

Papa's inventions were getting better too. He had developed a metal strip he called a HUD-DEE to go around kitchen sinks so water didn't run through and the material used for the counter tops didn't rot out. He was good at inventing but not so good at business. He was still working for Sears and Roebuck. The bosses convinced him that he would always have a job with them but they wanted to own the patents. Foolishly, he sold the patents for pennies of their real worth. He thought it made better sense just to have a job all the time. He continued to invent just about as much as he continued to drink. A lot of the money he got for the inventions was spent in the tavern before he ever got the money back home for the family to use.

CHAPTER SEVEN:

His children adored him and Mama loved him as much as the first time she met him. She had written him letters even before the children were born, whenever he was out of town on a job.

***

My Cherie:

Honey, you go where ever you think best and it will be all right with me. As for trusting you - you know, Bill, I trust you absolutely - I couldn't love you very much if I didn't - where there is no trust, there is no respect and where no respect - there is no love --See? I know, dear, you've always played fair - that's one of the loveable things about you - So you think I could have a man who lied to me - or did worse? Do you think I could give all of me to such a person - No - I have all the confidence in the world in you, *Cherie,* and always let it be that way.
I try so hard to understand you and I'm happy if you think I do - for you are a very odd sort of "guy", my Bill - but a most wonderful one too. Just so wonderful that no one else could ever take your place.

11-

I would have answered yesterday, honey, but didn't have any stamps – am I forgiven? Did you get the letter I sent to you to the restaurant? I don't want you to leave, sweetheart, without me seeing you. I wouldn't like that – do you think you could manage to come down here? Try hard. And never worry about me trusting you, dear. I do. And as someone had said "it's greater to be trusted – more of a compliment – than to be loved." Let me hear from you, honey, as soon as possible or rather be real sweet and come down.

I like to hear you say *"it's morning* and remember, dear, **"into each life some rain must fall,"** some days must be dark and dreary, just you think of what is to be and of how I love you – for I do, Bill – with all that's in me. I love you with a thousand kisses,

Your own, Jo.

(Written by Josephine Hill ....1922)

CHAPTER EIGHT: 1942

Pattie Jean had grown up right before Mama's eyes. Mama was very proud of her first-born daughter. Pattie Jean was turning into a beautiful young woman. She was slender with long dark hair, flawless skin, and a little beauty mark by her right eye. She has a few beaus too. She went to the movies and to school dances. She had many friends. She loved her family and always wanted to spend time with them.

The United States was getting involved with World War II and factories were hiring women to work. Pattie Jean was going to graduate from high school. She wanted to help with the war effort because she could make some good money. She knew she could help her family out with the cost of raising the big family as well.

She also had another idea. She especially wanted to get out of the house. She really wanted to move to California, Land of the Sun, warm temperatures and ....**Hollywood**! Aunt Lucille had already moved to California. She was married and had a daughter only a few years younger than Pattie Jean. Her daughter's name was Norma and she looked just like a movie star in the Photoplay magazine that

Pattie Jean loved to read. Pattie Jean decided to try to get a job in a local factory to earn some money. She found out she would need her birth certificate to prove her age. She looked around the apartment in all of the old boxes but came up empty.

Finally, she got the nerve to ask Mama where her birth certificate was. Mama said she would have to write to the State of Oklahoma for the certificate. She told Pattie Jean the name of the town where she was born; Okmulgee, Oklahoma on January 11, 1924. Mama got a really bad headache after Pattie Jean asked about the birth certificate. Mama said Pattie Jean had to write for the birth certificate herself because Mama didn't want to have anything to do with it.

Pattie Jean just couldn't understand why Mama got so upset about it. She just wanted the birth certificate so she could get a job; why was that making Mama angry?

THE EARLY YEARS...

Pattie Jean came from a long line of strong female ancestors. Her mother, **Josephine** Crim, was born on October 22, 1901 in Coles County, Il. She married Arthur Tecumseh Hill (born on 11-2-1897) on August 31, 1919 in Okmulgee, OK. She wasn't even 18 years old when she married and moved to Oklahoma. She moved away from her entire family and all her friends who lived in Illinois.

Mary Elizabeth Nation (center) mother to Anna Mae Alice Smith ((right side) - 1892

Pattie Jean's grandmother was **Anna Mae Alice Smith** (born Jan. 1872 – Coles County, Il. Alice married Charles H. Crim (born June, 1871 – Charleston, Il.) on May 28, 1891 in Charleston, IL. They had several children as was the custom at that time. First born was Bessie in 1892, Gage in 1894, Henry in 1895, Orlie in 1897, Mary in 1898, and Harold in 1900.

The story goes that Charles expected strict obedience from his wife and children. Alice's job was to keep house, cook, do laundry, and raise the children. Apparently, Charles also believed that Alice was just another possession. He was a businessman. His company was the Charleston Ice Cream Cone Company and it was a financial success.

In late 1901, Charles met another woman and decided to divorce Alice. His statement on the divorce papers claimed that Alice had been unfaithful because she got pregnant with another baby. The baby would turn out to be Josephine. He threw Alice out during her pregnancy and she went back home to live with her parents. In the Court records of the divorce, Charles claimed an adulterous relationship between **Alice Smith Crim** and James W. Dawson. Charles got an uncontested divorce and was able to retain the sole custody of the first 6 children. Alice was to have no contact with any of her children. The children ranged in age from 9 years down to 2 years. Can you imagine how upsetting it was for those children to be separated from their mother and for Alice not to be with her young children?

The divorce was granted on Sept. 2, 1901 and Charles married Bertha Kerns six weeks later! It makes one wonder just who was unfaithful.

Alice was over 7 months pregnant with Josephine but Charles denied being the father. Josephine was never listed in any CRIM family records either. Alice Smith Crim lived with her parents during the rest of her pregnancy. It is unknown how and when Alice Smith Crim came to meet James Dawson. She had been the mother of 6 children and she was a homemaker. It is difficult to understand how she would have the time to meet another man and have an affair.

It is further unknown if she had any relationship with James Dawson prior to becoming pregnant with Josephine. But they did live in the same town. In all probability, her parents were acquainted with the Dawson family.

Records on the Dawsons indicate that a William Dawson fought in the Revolutionary War, and his son, George Wiley Dawson, was killed in the Civil War. George Wiley Dawson was married to Nancy. After George's death, his widow, Nancy Dawson and children moved to Illinois. Nancy Dawson was living at 103 W. Walnut, Charleston, IL. (According to the 1900 census) with a son, James Wiley Dawson, who was 46 and divorced. Two of James's brothers moved to California between 1900 and 1910.

James Wiley Dawson was born on the 4th of July, 1854. He was a policeman in Charleston, IL. Perhaps that is how he became acquainted with Alice's family. After James and Alice were married and had children, times were tough. James retired from the police department because of his health. Then James decided to go to California to visit his brothers and possibly find work. He remained there for about six months and died there on Aug. 15, 1922. His body was shipped back to Charleston and he was buried in the Mound Cemetery in Illinois.

No record of a marriage certificate between James Wiley Dawson and **Anna Mae Alice Smith Crim Dawson** has been located. There were lots of different ways that Alice Smith used her legal name so it is possible the marriage certificate is listed differently or they might have been married in another city. James was 46 years old and Alice was 28 years of age when they first lived together at 103 W. Walnut with his mother, Nancy.

After Nancy's death in 1911, James and Alice continued to live in the same house raising their children. After James's death on Aug. 15, 1922, Alice Smith Crim Dawson started her own business running a boarding house at the same address. Josephine was born on October 22, 1901. No birth certificate has been located to confirm if she was named as Crim or Dawson. Old neighbors did recall Josephine and believed her last name was Dawson. A former tenant at the boarding house between 1919 and 1920 remembered her along with her younger sister, Lucille (born April 17, 1905) and a brother, James Leonard Dawson (born Nov. 18, 1911). Another boy baby had been born on Feb. 29, 1908 and died on March 7, 1908, named Luther Raye Dawson. After James Dawson's death, Alice Smith Crim Dawson struggled to raise three children alone.

Josephine and sister Lucille - 1907

According to the 1918 census, Josephine Dawson lived at 103 W. Walnut with her mother and worked at the Charleston Cone Plant. The Cone Plant was owned by Charles Crim! It appears that Alice and Josephine must have discussed Alice's past relationship, including her first marriage to Charles Crim, because Josephine mentioned her grandfather, Rufus Crim, in a diary in later years. Even more interesting is that Josephine was hired by the Charleston Cone Plant in spite of the fact that Charles Crim had denied being her father. Could Charles Crim have had some remorse for denying this child?

THE CRIM FAMILY

Rufus Crim (born Nov. 1844 in Delphi, Indiana) married Lydia Brusmon (born 1850 in Illinois) on May 9, 1866 in Coles County, IL. They had six sons, one of which was **Charles**. In his later years, after 1904, Rufus was in and out of a mental hospital in Kankakee, IL.

JOSEPHINE DAWSON - 1920's

Josephine was born on October 22, 1901. She had dark hair and dark eyes and was full of life. She grew into a very pretty young lady. She was an incurable romantic with a flair for the dramatic. She wrote stories and poems and expressed herself in any written way she could. Surely, she would have been a 1920's flapper if she could have found her way to the speak-easy taverns with all that wonderful music playing.

Instead she used her creative outlets by writing limericks and poems.

"You tell -em salad, - I'm dressing!"
"You tell 'em pony - I'm horse!"
"You tell -em cricket - Katy did!"
"You tell 'em photograph - You've got the record!
  ***
"The thing that goes the farthest towards making life worthwhile...
that costs the least... and does the most... is just a pleasant smile"
  ***
"When I am dying, lean over me tenderly
Stoop as the yellow roses droop in the wind from the South.
So I may -when I awake- if there be an awakening
Keep what lulled me to sleep - the touch of your lips on my mouth"
  ***
"Bananas are yellow, watermelon cut thick…You'd better write me pretty damn quick!"

***

Call me back – Pal of mine
Let me dream once again
Call me back – to your heart – Pal of mine
Let me roam once again down in old Lover's lane
As I did in the days gone by...
Let me live in your arms
Let me thrill with your charms
Let me kiss those sweet lips so divine
Let me gaze in your eyes where I'll find Paradise
Call me back to your heart – Pal of mine"

***

Phil and Bill are a pair of twins
Alike in looks and coos.
When Ma gives them their little baths
Sometimes poor Bill gets two!

***

The **"U"** stands for the Union eternal
The **"S"** for the Stripes and Stars
The **"A"** for the Army undefeated
The victor in a dozen wars,
The **"U"** stands for Uncle Sammy
The **"S"** for our Ships in stern array
The **"A"** for the Almighty One who guards us.
That's the meaning of **U-S-A!**

***

*All that's beautiful is seen... in bewitching Josephine.
And what a world would living mean...
with a girl like Rosaleen
Seems like life would be divine...
with a girl like Madeline*
 ***
*A youth who lived over in Corning
Said the girls always start me scorning
At night they fake-up a wonderful make-up
But, gosh, they look tough in the morning!*
 ***
*Mary had a swarm of bees
She loved their buzzing lives
They, too, loved their Mary cause
Their Mary had the hives!*
 ***
*Mary had a little lamb when first she came to town
And Mary was a modest girl and wore a long, long gown.
But styles of dress are changing now; her gown is cut in half.
Who cares a damn for Mary's lamb – when Mary shows her calf?*
 ***

Josephine's husband – Arthur T. Hill's family background.

John Tillman Hill (born Oct. 17, 1856 in Cumberland County, IL. He married Louisa Florence Oldham (born August 28, 1859 in Wabash, IN.) on February 9, 1882 also in Cumberland County, IL. They had six children. Walter, Leota Maude, Sadie Minnie, Grace, Belvia, and **Arthur.**

The first son, Walter, became a carpenter and builder and moved to Okmulgee, OK. His youngest brother, **Arthur**, moved with him. After a few years, Walter developed Parkinson's disease and could no longer work. He returned with his family to Illinois. His wife left him and moved from Illinois to find work. After two or three years, the children joined her. Walter killed himself at his sister Grace's house in the early 1930s, probably due to depression and poor health.

Arthur remained working in Okmulgee. He returned to Charleston for a short time and married **Josephine Crim Dawson** on August 31, 1919. They moved back to Okmulgee, Oklahoma but Josephine often returned to Illinois to visit her in-laws and her own family.

<u>Arthur T. Hill and Josephine - 1919</u>

Josephine never seemed to settle down in Okalahoma. She always was searching for something else. She was restless and felt there was a life much more exciting out there somewhere for her.

It was the early days of Arthur and Josephine Hill's marriage...in 1919. Arthur was a serious and very hard-working man. He had built up a good reputation for an honest day's work in Okmulgee. His jobs were plentiful enough to support him and he was determined to keep his family in a decent home and have plenty of food. He was a quiet and thoughtful man who kept his problems to himself. He didn't seem to have much in common with his choice of a wife like Josephine. He didn't seem to understand what Josephine needed and wanted from him as a husband and as the children's father in later years.

Josephine was an excellent cook, she could sew; she kept a clean house and managed very well with the money he provided. She had learned her skills from her mother working in the boarding house. After all, you couldn't run a good boarding house unless you kept the boarders well fed and provided clean rooms. Josephine also loved to listen to the radio, go to the picture show, and she read anything she could get her hands on – whether it was the newspaper or a magazine or a book.

She learned to keep herself busy during the day when Arthur was working. She made some of their clothing and was quite skilled in sewing without a pattern. She also prepared Arthur's lunches every day. Occasionally, she would walk to his job site, if it was nearby, to spend a few minutes with him. She longed to talk and gossip and dream about the future and even if Arthur wasn't really listening, she was happy to be with him.

If she wasn't writing poems and limericks, she was cutting poems out of the newspaper and pasting them in a scrapbook to keep and to reread over and over. She was truly a dreamer. She was also an avid letter writer. She kept in touch with her sister, Lucille, whom she sometimes referred to as Cindy. Lucille and their young brother, James Leonard, still lived with Alice in Charleston and kept the boarding house going as well as they could.

Josephine went home to visit a few times. She missed the bigger city and her old friends and most especially her family. She would also spend a few days with her in-laws and bring them news of Arthur's work and how well he provided for his family. She was very proud of her husband but.....she was often lonely.

Arthur was sure once the children started coming that Josephine would settle down and become so busy raising the babies that she would forget about the silly dreams she had.

Josephine and Arthur Hill, Okmulgee, OK - 1920

When Josephine gave birth to their first child, a son named James Leonard, on July 11, 1920, Arthur was sure that life would now be perfect. Josephine adored her little Jimmie. He was named after her young brother and she sang and talked and hugged and kissed him most of the day. But she was still lonely. When Jimmie was asleep and Arthur was still working and all her housework was completed, she wrote poems and dreamed of what might be.

    She was sure there had to be more to life than this. She would not trade her husband or her baby son for anything but...still... She felt a restlessness that she could not put aside.
***

BABY BOY

I think God took the midnight blue
To make my Jimmie's eyes.
And little stars to twinkle too
When baby laughs or cries.
I think God took a wee dove's coo
To make my baby's words
They sound so much alike those two;
God's babies and God's birds.
I think God took a Lily white
To make my Jimmie's skin
They are so delicate and white
Just like my baby's skin
I think God took the laughter
And all the other joys
For my own earthly happiness
God made my Jimmie boy.

Written 1921 by Josephine Hill
   ***

Josephine became the mother of a baby boy but her days of romance and drama were far from over...

Arthur's work was becoming more demanding. He had to hire a man to do the house painting on his job sites. They struck up a friendship. Bill Drain was a good man. He was originally asked by Walter Hill to come to Oklahoma and work. He was ambitious, clever, hard working, and a fellow that most people liked to have around. He was single and loved to travel around the country looking for work and learning new crafts. He considered himself a bit of an inventor and was always working on some little gadget he made out of scraps he found along the way.

Naturally, Arthur soon invited Bill to come home for a good meal. He was pleased to see how well Bill got along with Josephine and even with little Jimmie. Bill seemed to enjoy the family setting and spent many hours with the three members of the Hill family. Arthur was happy to show Bill what a real family could mean to him and how wonderful it was to be the man of the family and provide well for those that he loved. Arthur was sure that if Bill found the right woman, he would settle down too. Maybe the two men could even become business partners in the future.

A couple of years passed by and it wasn't long before Josephine was pregnant again. She had a hard time carrying this pregnancy and was often tired. She gained more weight and had to rest more often but she continued to keep her house and her family well fed and content.

On January 11, 1924, Josephine and Arthur became the very proud parents of twins....a boy and a girl. They named the children Jackie Jo and Pattie Jean. The twins were fraternal. They shared many of the same physical characteristics but they were a typical boy and girl in their mannerisms and interests. Josephine was thrilled to have a little brother for Jimmie to play with and she was especially happy to have a daughter. She was soon making little outfits for Pattie Jean and loved to dress her up like a little doll. Pattie Jean was a tiny girl but very pretty and sweet.

Josephine and twin babies - 1924

It was a few months later that something unexpected occurred. Josephine became aware that she was strongly attracted to Bill. She had enjoyed his company before the twins came along. She thought of him as a good friend to both Arthur and herself. He was happy to run errands and help around their home. He was entertaining. He told lots of stories and sang plenty of songs. He played with the children. It was like having a brother close by.

But now, she realized that she thought about him all the time. She tried to see him as much as possible. She knew it was wrong but she was drawn to him like a moth to a flame.

Bill had the same feelings. He left town for weeks at a time to find other work. He traveled to other cities in an effort to stay away from Josephine but he was not able to get her out of his mind. He would return and work with Arthur, go to dinner with Arthur's family, play with the children, and treasure his moments with Josephine. He was feeling very confused about what was happening. Arthur was a dear friend and Bill was not sure what to do.

Josephine finally told Arthur that she was not happy staying in Okmulgee. She wanted to go back to Charleston to be with her family. Her mother, Alice was ill and Josephine wanted to help out with the boarding house, spend time with her sister and brother, and take the children to meet their grandparents, including Arthur's family. She thought if she was away from Arthur, she could think more clearly about what she really wanted out of her life. Possibly, she could get Bill out of her mind and heart too.

Bill volunteered to take them back and help her with the children during the travel home. It didn't take long before Josephine realized that she wanted to spend more time with Bill to see what her feelings really meant.

A change was coming.....and it might be the beginning of the end.....

***

I want a friend who'll some day be
A great deal more than a "friend" to me
Someone whose heart is big and true
Someone, old dear, just like you!
***
Bread is dry; Butter is greasy
I love you kid; don't get uneasy!
***
Apples in the cellar; Peaches on the shelf
I am getting awful tired; of sleeping by myself.
***

A Question

If all this world was good and true
And in this world there were but two
And you knew that no one else knew
Would you?
If all this world was good and bright
And if I stayed with you all night
And if I turned out the lights...
Would you?
If we were in a certain place
And we were lying face to face
Nothing between us but some space
Would you?

***

Candy is sweet; but sugar is sweeter
I would like awfully well; to be your little housekeeper.

***

Sooner or later, you'll forget
All you are saying tonight...and yet...
Tis sweet for the stars to kiss the sea
But not half as sweet as you're kissing me.
It doesn't mean a thing I know
But I like your line ...and so...
The moonlight has a thousand charms
As I lie content in your warm young arms
Kiss my fingers, my hair and eyes
Whisper a thousand precious lies
Kiss my neck, my arms and then...
Kiss my trembling lips again.

Love me, hold me just tonight
Till the stars are turning white
Sooner or later, you'll soon forget
All you're saying tonight and yet...

***

Gee, I feel blue. The hours seem just like years to me. Don't know what to do. I have nothing but memories. Days are dark and lonely. I hear the blues in every song; you are always on my mind. I wonder what will become of me? Because I have tried everything but you're tired of everything I do.
 And so...
Evening brings the twilight.
The nightingale at starlight,
But all it brings me is just a memory.
I'm tired of being alone
And waiting by the telephone.
I'm even tired of the moon above
I guess it's just because
I'm in love.
I'm tired of everything but you.

Written by Josephine Hill
***

In 1919, during the time Josephine had left her Illinois home to live with Arthur in marriage in Oklahoma, her mother, Alice continued to run the boarding house in Illinois. Alice hired some help in exchange for room and board. She also had Lucille (born

in 1905) and James Leonard (born in 1910) still at home. Of course, both the children helped to care for the chickens, collect the eggs, and do other chores around the home. Alice also began complaining more often about her headaches. There were some days that she stayed in bed for hours. When Josephine would go home, she would help her mother run the boarding house. It was obvious during that time that Alice had become seriously ill. In 1923, Alice was nearly bedridden because the pain in her head was becoming almost constant. Often she made little sense and didn't know her own children.
   The doctors put her into the mental hospital for a period of time believing that she was losing her mind.
   Anna Mae Alice Smith Crim Dawson died on February 21, 1923 at the age of 51. The cause of death was later diagnosed as a brain tumor. Her father was Charles Smith of Canada and her mother was Mary Elizabeth Nation of Indiana. There is some belief that she was descended from an Indian tribe but no connection has been confirmed as of this date. She was buried at Mound Cemetery in Charleston, IL. beside her husband, James Wiley Dawson. Josephine was 23 years old,

Lucille was 17 years old and James Leonard was 13 years old.

Josephine, her mother Alice and son Jimmie Hill - 1922

At the time of her mother's death, Josephine had only her first born son, Jimmie, who was not even 3 years old. She went back to Charleston to help settle the affairs of her mother. This was a traumatic time period for Alice's children, especially James Leonard. He was fostered out to a farm family named Craig. James Leonard had lived with his mother and sisters all his life. James Leonard learned plenty on the farm and in fact, he became a farmer in his adult years. He always loved animals and was very skillful in using farm equipment and planting crops. However, he used to beg his sisters to let him come live with them. His sweet mood seemed to change. His sisters thought it was because he had to grow up. He was living away from his family and he had to learn to be a man. Like the rest of his family, he was a very hard worker. He had always liked to work outside and he was learning new skills. Skills that would be with him for the rest of his life.

THE BEGINNING OF THE END – 1926 ***

How many times have I undertaken to make you play on the square?
Day after day I've been crying – wondering if you care.
Hour after hour I've been trying to lay the blame on you.
Cause I might have known, I'd be left all alone
Because the love you've shown is proved untrue.
Time after time I wished you could be mine
But fate has been so unkind.
That's why I am lonely.
But some day I may forget that we ever met and go alone....
I might have known.

Possibly written by Bill Drain to Josephine Hill about 1925. The handwriting was different than Josephine's.
***

In 1925, Josephine left her husband again and traveled to Chicago, IL. She told her husband that she needed to check on her sister, Lucille, and her brother, James Leonard. She found a room with cooking privileges on Wilson Avenue for herself and the twins. Apparently she left Jimmie, her oldest child, with Arthur in Oklahoma. The twins were a year old. Her sister, Lucille, was living nearby. Bill was staying with Josephine when he was in town. He was still traveling around the country looking for work. Arthur was sending Josephine money from time to time but Josephine's life was tough. Arthur still wanted his wife to return to Okalahoma and for the entire family to live together. He wasn't ready to give up on his marriage.

Josephine received a Christmas gift of a 1926 diary from Lucille in 1925.
* * *

Jan 1, 1926: First day of the New Year-didn't awake till late. Just messed around. Bill took Pattie Jean out for an airing down to Lucille's. I journeyed downtown myself about 5 P.M. Sent telegram to Arthur in Oklahoma. Ate chili-was good and then home at nine. Jean and Lucille and I went over on Sedgwick Ave. to see about that job-go back in the morning- one of *"gotta do something.- things are looking mighty serious* but...it's always bleakest before dawn so why worry - worry don't get you anything but wrinkles!"

Jan 2: Oh Lord! What a day! Lucille came down and we went to see about that job. Came back and Pattie Jean had a spasm or something-was over at the doctor's office. I was so frightened-she looked as if she was dead. Doctor was mean, wouldn't give us the prescription cause we didn't have the two dollars! Received Arthur's telegram-decided to go to Charleston. Came back to room and those crazy Scottish boys came. We had to go to the show with them and the blonde and Belle. Gee-my head hurts so-came back and Lucille and I had a round. She is done with me because I love Bill. *I do love him*. She leaves for Charleston in the morning. I have both the kiddies-what next?

Jan 3: Nothing much happened today. Up about ten-had breakfast-Jean came up and took Jackie Jo down to her room. Lucille never went to Charleston-decided to wait till next Sunday. Thinks she'll get work- I doubt it. Brother James Leonard was out to visit and Jackie Jo came back. I went to the store-ate chili. I sure love that stuff. Then those Scotch "pests" came up. And the big blonde one-she was telling me about her kids-hasn't seen them in seven years! Bill says she's a "dope head". I don't know. Rained all day-kids tore all my pictures down-climbed up and got them off the fireplace-just think of it!

Jan 4: Nothing new! Lucille came up. Landed a job at Bedells and goes to work in the morning. Took Jackie Jo home with her this afternoon. James Leonard brought him back tonight. Nothing new-just another day. No word from Arthur.

Jan 5: Same old stuff-just another day-no word yet from Arthur. Lucille and Jess came down tonight. Lucille and I took a walk to North Ave. Bill looked for a job this morning. Nothing doing.

Jan 6: Pat was sick last night. Poor Bill cleaned all night it seemed. I don't know what's wrong with Pattie Jean. We (Bill & I) got some castor oil down her, perhaps that will straighten her out. Gee! I'm so lonesome and blue. My Bill is gone- left this morning for Springfield, IL. It hurt to see him go but something had to be done. Went down to Lucille's and got supper for her. She likes her work so well, got a raise! 18 cents per hour now! Jess & her helped me home with the kiddies. No word from Arthur. Lucille said she ought to hear from him and get an answer to her letter. *I wonder what she has told him.* I'll write him myself tonight. – OH! I wish my Bill was here – it's so terrible lonesome without him. **I love him so.**

Jan 7: Just another day-nothing new. No word from Arthur yet –Every thing seems all wrong. I miss my Bill so I wonder where he is tonight. Is he thinking of me? (I love you, Bill- I love you!) P.S. Lucille spoke her mind when she learned my watch was pawned!

Jan 8: I miss my Bill so! No word from anyone. Bill or Arthur either. Surely I'll hear tomorrow. Pattie Jean has been so cross today and she looks so bad; I am worried so about her. I found out what is wrong with her tonight. That old Doc told Beulah-internal hemorrhage. I can't think what caused it. He was so mean- wouldn't tell us what to do for the poor little thing. I do hope I hear from Bill tomorrow and Arthur too. Everything seems so "balled up" maybe I just think so because I've got the blues. Think I'll read some of Bill's old letters.

Jan 9: Well, no word from my Bill yet. I'm so worried-he promised he'd write the next day. He has just been gone two days but Lordy! It seems like years-does he miss me like that? I wonder: can a man care like a woman? I doubt it very much. For me, there is no one like "my boy" now or anytime. Received a letter from Arthur-it sounded like he didn't receive my night letter-poor fellow. I hate to keep asking him for money but what else can I do? It's for the kiddies. Lucille purchased herself some new pumps and a dress. I've got to make an arrangement with the landlord in the morning. No money, Lord, I wish it was over.

Jan. 10: Been down to Lucille's all day-waited around up in the room for that darn old landlord. Came back here about six and tried to call him again but he was out. Jess helped me down with my suitcases. We just saved clothes, hope I get some mail tomorrow.

Jan. 11: Today is the twins' birthday. They're two years old, bless their hearts – how time flies! Rec'd two letters from my boy, he is at Bloomington. I just wonder when we'll ever be together again-I can't ask him to take the responsibility of my kiddies. He is just a boy himself - but - I can't give him up either. What can we do? I want him so and my babies too. Got a letter from Arthur- he is so good. Lucille heard from Flora-she is married to Raymond-an old sweetie of mine. She just took him for a meal ticket-he is a good kid. Oh Lordy, we all been talking about babies being born-Lucille and Jean and I know all there is to know about that! Yes sir!

Jan. 12: Nothing new happened today...the twins went calling up to Mrs. Jones on the third floor, and then fell back down the back stairs! Lucille and I went over to Beulah's a while tonight. She and Lucille sympathize with one another...both in the same boat! Wish MY BILL was here.

Jan. 13: Lucille and I went down to Bedells this morning. Lunched at Woolworths. I went down to see about my trunk this evening. Gee, the man was so nice, said he thought my husband had run away and left me! Read about "Luipe" in the American tonight showed his picture...he is a good kid. Hope he does make the big league -think I'll write him a line.

That wouldn't be disloyal to MY BILL for it's just BILL I love always. Got the sweetest letter from him yesterday, he was going to Springfield. If nothing was there, on to St. Louis. Hope my man writes me tomorrow.

Jan. 14: Didn't get up till late today...just fooled around. Got a letter from Arthur... sent me three dollars. I got my laundry out and then ironed this evening. Beulah came over tonight. Lucille told her about that candy and Lord! Harry was listening. They sure are having Hell now! No letter from Bill -I wonder where he is?

Jan. 15: Well, we all had a wild night last night. Lucille and Jess took turns "feeding the fish". And then Beulah was sick on the second floor – guess she'll do it by tomorrow morning. No letter.

Jan. 16: Got a letter from Arthur but no telegram -don't know whether we'll make it to Charleston tomorrow. Hope so. This way is getting on my nerves. Don't know whether Beulah did any good or not; we all have been having a discussion. Jess & Lucille and I. I think I've proved to everybody's satisfaction that I love Bill honest and truly. Just wish he was here. No letter (why don't he write?)

Jan. 17: Just a blue old Sunday, never heard from Arthur. Jess sent telegram at noon. We've just got to go to Charleston but how? We ate Eskimo pies and popcorn just a while ago and before that – chili. That is all we done...eat and sleep. What will tomorrow bring forth? These are thrilling days...

To give the readers an explanation of what all the above diary entries might have meant...

Josephine had left Arthur and her first born son in Okmulgee, OK. She went back to IL. with Bill to figure out what she wanted. She had the twins and was spending time with her sister, Lucille, in a rooming house. Money was extremely tight. She was asking Arthur to send money for the twins' needs. Bill was out of town looking for work. Lucille had a boyfriend, Jess, and she was trying to help care for the twins. Josephine was truly still wanting her romantic dream and hoping for the best. James Leonard, her half-brother, did come to visit occasionally. I believe, (based on future occurrences) that James Leonard was being physically and possibly sexually abused by Arthur Craig, the farm owner. I believe James Leonard wanted to tell his sisters but was too embarrassed. I also believe that James Leonard had begun sexually abusing Pattie Jean when she was less than two years of age which caused the internal hemorrhage that the Doctor mentioned when Pattie Jean was sick. I think Josephine may have suspected that James Leonard was being abused by Mr. Craig but didn't know how to handle the situation. Josephine dearly loved both her sister and brother and felt responsible for them. I don't believe she knew that James Leonard was abusing her daughter. I also believe that Lucille and Beulah were pregnant and swallowed something to cause a miscarriage (entries Jan. 15, 16, 18, and 19).

The diary continues: 1926

Jan. 18, 1926: Well, no word yet from Arthur. We got to get out. Think Harry has rented these rooms. Oh Lord! I'm so worried about several things - how we are going to come out? Got a card from Bill from St. Louis, said he was going to

Springfield, MO. Took the kiddies out for a walk down Clark St. to the Post Office. Went up and seen Beulah; she is so much better...guess she'll come out of it all right now.

Jan. 19: Nothing new today. Beulah done her stuff and...Oh! I never realized just what it all meant until I looked at that. Never again will I do anything like that! Wrote Arthur a letter...poor fellow. I just know he thinks I'm terrible. He can't think anything else hardly. Lucille is so sick...has been in bed all day today. It just doesn't seem right for women to have all the suffering during such a period and then so much of it during the "windup".

Jan. 20: No letter from anyone today. Lucille still sick, been in bed for two days. Durkin, the man who killed some FBI agents in Chicago has been captured after so long a time. He has sure got nerve. I admire that in a man like him. Went down to Dolly's Laundry on Pierson to see about our "embroidered linen" lunch cloth. Laundry man from Wilson was over collecting...coming back tomorrow for his money. **I'm not in!**

Jan. 21: Got a letter from Arthur and one from Bill. Arthur sent me a money order and what a time I had trying to cash it. Harry had to go with me around to the drug store. Bill is in Ohio...said he would see me Sunday. I sure hope so. Been such a long time since he was here. Went and had my hair cut to begorra! I wish I knew what was going to be. Guess we'll leave Sat. for Charleston. What a scare I had last night!

Jan. 22: Five below last night. Gee, but it was cold. Jackie Jo woke up twice froze! I cooked butter beans and pork shoulder today and made a strawberry short cake. It tasted so good! Reckon we will leave tomorrow for Charleston at six. Lord, what a trip with Lucille and I like we are. Gosh, but it's cold!

Jan. 23. Didn't get to write in this yesterday, too much other stuff. Left Chicago yesterday at four...Six degrees, Lord, was it cold! Lucille was sick. Got in Mattoon at 10:25 and met Bill Armstrong and Zollie O'Hair. Laid over two hours, kids crying and everything! Met Owen Water as we stepped off, registered at Clover Lake. Andrew Sullivan was head clerk... what a room! And Bill walked in on us; put the kiddies to bed at three. Charleston is just the same.

Jan. 24: Rose at ten, took Lucille her breakfast, met Brendan and Sadie Mills. Bill and I ate and then Cindy (Lucille) and I took a stroll down to Wilsons. Learned all the latest gossip. James looks the same, met Tommy at the pool hall, stopped at Stan's to phone, went over to Mrs. Tutt. Agreed about room, back to the hotel. Lucille laid down. I went out to see their rooms, rented them. Met Bill uptown, ate, and then got Lucille to move out. Bill got Denny, he came over.

Jan. 25: Went for walk and came back. Lucille took Jackie Jo and went over to Ruth Collins. Ought to write Arthur and would but haven't a stamp now nor any money. Lucille is reading some of Denny's old letters.

Jan. 26: Bill here, left for Springfield and then came back about four, changed his route. Denny came over before supper.

Jan. 27: Nothing new Denny and Lucille went to town.

Jan. 29: Lucille and Jackie Jo went over to Ruth C. to spend the day. Ray brought the groceries out.

Jan. 30: No letter. Bill came over, landed a job in Mattoon. Called James Leonard but he couldn't come in. Denny and Lucille gone to the dance. I can't think how all of this will end.

Jan. 31: This has sure been one gloomy old day. Bill left at eleven and Lucille and Henry Lewis went for a ride. Sure was one long lonesome day. Jess sent Lucille a special delivery. Lord, but I wish I knew how everything will turn out.

Feb.1: No word from Arthur – beginning to look as if he was going back on me. The old lady here is scared to death she isn't going to get her money. Jess wired Lucille five dollars and we owe twenty-five. Denny came by from work. Gee, I feel punk tonight, wish Bill would call.

Feb. 2: Rec'd letter from Bill on his way to Parsons, Kansas. Wind up at Tulsa. Denny took me down to the Post Office. Two letters from Arthur. No wonder I didn't hear from him... sent them Special. Denny brought some books down, had a nice evening reading. Lucille gone and kids all asleep!

Feb. 3: Lucille sick all day, called Dr. Craig tonight, he came out twice and gave her a hypo. Denny came past, going to town. I'm so tired.

Feb. 4: Lucille not any better, called Doctor again tonight. Rec'd such a nice letter from Arthur. He is a good man. Denny came by, Lucille has been after me all day to buy ice over at the store. Wonder if Bill is at Parsons?

Feb.5: Seemed like spring today. Rec'd a letter from Arthur, but none from my Bill. I do wish he was here. If it's a girl, I think it shall be called "Billie". I read a story about a girl named that!
    ***
This passion is but an ember of a sun;
Of a fire that has been set.
I could not live and remember; And so I love and forget.
(Shall I do that some day?) I love you, Bill..

Feb. 6: No letter from anyone today. Jess wired Lucille ten dollars. Ruth Covley came over. She and Lucille went to town. And now Lucille is going to the dance. Been in bed for three days... now going up there! Denny gone to take his wife over to her Mother's. Called James Leonard, he talks so funny. Said he would try and come in tomorrow. The roads are so bad. I'm so tired but wish I was going to a dance. Haven't been to one since I left Oklahoma. "I want to go where he goes, do what he does, Love when he loves....then I'll be happy".

Feb. 7: Bill has been gone a week. I miss him so. Went down town this evening for a "Smart Set". Saw Cy Wallers and Mr. Craig. Mr. Craig walked out on Sixth with me. Wish Bill was here. I want him. Jackie Jo wants to sleep in his new overalls!

Feb. 8: Letter from Arthur but...Oh... what a letter. Doesn't think much of my proposition about moving to Tulsa and wants me to come back on certain conditions. Haven't heard a line from Bill yet. Don't know where he is. Just wish he was with me. Things would seem a little brighter anyway. My head hurts so I reckon I have the flu.

Feb. 9: Rec'd the money from Arthur, also his letter. Wrote and told him "YES", no other way I can see. Been so cold, snowing all day. Denny came past. He and Lucille drove to town to get me a Photoplay.

Feb. 10: Nothing new, nearly froze all day, no heat. Old man got two ton of coal this afternoon so reckon we all will get thawed out sometime. Can't imagine why I don't hear from Bill? Lucille all dressed, waiting for Denny to go to the dance. Me?...BED for mine.

Feb. 11: James Leonard came down today about 12:30. He is so big but still the same old James Leonard for all that. Hadn't seen him for three months. He is staying all night. Poor kid hates to go back to the old woman out there. He is so cranky. I wish I could take him home with me. He is going to make a fine man!

Feb. 12: No mail. I do wish I knew...lots of things. I reckon Bill has decided not to write, perhaps it is best now that I have decided to go back to Okmulgee but....oh! James Leonard went back out this afternoon, he hated to go so bad. He sure is a good kid. Denny came over. These days and nights...if something don't change very shortly, I am going to pass out.

Feb. 13: Bill in Tulsa, wonders why I don't write and I have wondered the same. Wrote him tonight, Denny will mail it out. He and Lucille going to the dance. It's raining, lonesome old night, how I long for my Bill. Don't look as if things will ever be right. I have done all I can do, I have no regrets along that line. (This is Bill's pencil I write with... bless his heart!)

Feb. 14. Sunday and gloomy one at that. Lucille rec'd a money order from Jess. Went to town to purchase some powder and rouge...first, we have had for a century! I went down to the College Inn for some sandwiches. Arthur Reis (one of the boys from around here) waits tables there. Came back and went to town for a book. Talked to Mickey David...wondered when I'll get my pumps out? Ted was here about three months ago, sure wish I could have seen him.

Feb. 15: Lucille went over to Ruth's. Arthur Baker seriously hurt in a holdup. Received a letter from Bill. He is back in Tulsa. Gibb working there too. I feel so bad so going to bed.

Feb. 16: Heard from Arthur. Sent me $17.00 and I owed nearly all of it! Purchased myself some ink. Denny came past and took Lucille to town. Little Jimmie was sick at home, sure hope he is alright now. Didn't get to get my pumps out.

Feb. 17: Lucille gone to the dance. Nothing happened much today. Rufus Crim died at Kankakee and Arthur Baker at Decatur. Am going to bed now, don't feel so good.

Feb. 18: Got a letter from Bill. Wonders why I don't write: I did. Answered with a long letter. Rained all day and is still at it...trying to sleet now. "This dreary weather makes me feel blue." (I can hear Bill singing that yet.)

Feb. 19: Got a letter from Arthur, bawling me out. I don't know what to do...don't believe we would stick long from the way he talked. Nothing new.

Feb. 20: Rec'd Special Delivery from Arthur. Also one from Bill. What a mess we all are in! How will it all end? Hansel Kackley married again, Eunice got left out again. Lucille is going to the dance, trying to slip away from Denny. She's got a date.

Feb. 21: Sunday-just another one. Lucille rec'd Special Delivery from Jess. Said he nearly burned himself up yesterday and was sick. Then a telegram came, she went to town, bought some sandwiches home and is gone again. I wrote Arthur; Gosh...these kids are driving me nuts.

Feb. 22: Lucille left today on the 10:29. Beulah called Mary Hammonds at 1:00 Monday morning. I don't think Jess is anyway near dangerously ill but perhaps he is. Delphia came out. Didn't know her. She is so big. Awfully nice girl though. The kids and I are going to bed. I'm tired out and it's so lonesome. Hope I get "stacks" of mail tomorrow.

Feb. 23: Ok, rec'd a letter from Bill. It's the beginning of the end. I reckon he thinks or he is trying to make himself believe that Jimmy D. is the same to me as he, when he knows better. There is no one but him but I can't convince him if he wants to believe otherwise.

Oh, My God ...to have it end like this. Tears are supposed to help one, I've wept barrels but where am I? <u>And the woman pays!</u> Denny came by, he is a good fellow. Said he would bring me a book tomorrow. Arthur wrote and said he had purchased himself a Stutz car. The Dark Angel is playing here. Bill and I saw that in Tulsa last fall, but those days are gone forever.

Feb. 24: Everything seems a little brighter...rec'd another letter from my Bill. I'm going to think he was drunk when he wrote the first one. He still is my Bill for all that. If Arthur will now only see it's best for me to go to Tulsa, the sun will be shining purty. I hope he does. Rec'd the laundry Jess sent from Chicago. James Leonard called; hope he gets to come in on Saturday.

Feb. 25: Another letter from Bill, he has seen his mistake but where are we? And what am I to do?

Feb. 26: A letter from Bill. Wants me to get a divorce and leave my babies in Okmulgee. Wish I knew what would be best? I've worried over it all 'till I am about cooked.

Feb. 27: Heard from Arthur and Bill both. Arthur expects me there and Bill wants me with him. I don't know...it's my babies or Bill.

NOTE TO DEAR READERS....

Please keep in mind that Josephine is 24 years old and Lucille is 20 years of age. I think you can see what I see. It appears that Lucille has a man who truly cares for her in Jess. But, apparently she is having fun with Denny (who sounds like a married man) and other old friends from the area. Lucille is probably pregnant too and sounds like the "morning sickness" got to her for a few weeks. She has gone back to Chicago to visit Jess after he got burned. Jess Woodward worked in and possibly even owned a carpet company.

Also, it appears that Josephine might be in the "family way" and the baby is certain to be Bill's. Josephine is still trying to have her fantasy romantic life by keeping Arthur hanging on in Oklahoma but not living with him. She adores her Bill and apparently has not told him of the pregnancy. So, there she is - away from her husband and not with her true love - **her man** -and trying to take care of her children with another baby on the way. She is trying to convince Arthur that she would be happier living in Tulsa because it is a bigger town...when in reality, she thinks she could see Bill more often when he is working there.

So....what will Josephine decide to do...?

THE DIARY CONTINUES.   FEB, 1926

Feb. 28: Another Sunday. Denny came by at noon and brought a paper for me to read and then came by tonight and helped pass away the time. It's so darn lonesome. James Leonard just called, poor kid, and wanted to know if I had talked to Arthur Craig? I wonder, would it be best to take him home with me or not? He is a good kid all right. Ike and Sam and Ora passed here this afternoon, more of the "eternal triangle".

Feb. 29: Wasn't anything. (Leap year)

March 1: Another letter from my Bill. He does want me and I'm beginning to think he cares now as I have always. "Awfulest" day, snow, rain and everything. March came in like a lion all right. The stork was worked to death Sunday night. Charlie Devore has a daughter (just makes about 4) Everett Meyers, a son (three) and Jay Rayans a son and Lordy knew how many more. Carrie Kearns married.

March 2: Letters from Arthur and Bill both. Arthur sent me some money, paid the rent and I am going to send for my trunk. He is so good. I can't see why everything has to be like this. Lucille wrote too, said she went to see The Dark Angel". It is so cold!

March 3: I'm slighted, not a line from a soul today. Wonder if Bill is sore at the proposition I made. I hope not. And, Arthur...I don't know what he'll think. I sure want to get away from here. It's so lonesome. Go to bed with the chickens, nothing else to do. Mrs. Charles Crim (She's the second wife and married Charles a few weeks after he had divorced Alice – Josephine's mother) said Mr. Crim is sick in a hospital in Auburn, In. Too bad. Haven't got to send for my trunk yet. I do wish Denny would come by. Bud Wrenns had a son.

March 4: Letter from Arthur. <u>He is DONE</u> the minute I go back to Bill. I can't have everything. Finally got my letter off to Lucille about my trunk. Sure will be glad when I get it, also my watch.

March 5: James Leonard came in today. Went to see Mr. Craig about going home with me. Mr. Craig just called out here, doesn't want James Leonard to go. James Leonard just called. Said he found something out about Mr. Craig wouldn't tell it over the phone. Hope he can come in tomorrow. Poor kid, I feel so sorry for him. Heard from Lucille. Jess is still sick.

Sent Denny a note. Denny came by, been working overtime. I'm worried about James Leonard. I suppose Mr. Craig has spent his money.

Dear Readers: *I am thinking that James Leonard might have received a little money from Alice's estate when the boarding house was sold. Mr. Craig was appointed as his guardian. Mr. Craig probably spent the money and doesn't want to have to return any of it if James Leonard leaves to live with one of his sisters.*

March 6: James Leonard didn't get to come in. Rained all day and is still doing it. Well, got a letter from Arthur last night. Said I couldn't go back to Bill as long as Arthur lived. I can't think. Didn't hear from Bill today. Denny came by last night, thought sure he never was going to leave. Stayed until 9 o'clock and I am always in bed by seven!

March 7: Sunday again. Just like any other day to me. Awfully cold. Tried to snow and everything. Purchased myself a Sunday paper this morning from some little boy. Just had eight cents but I got it. Do hope James Leonard gets to come in tomorrow and hope my trunk and watch arrive.

March 8: Rec'd three special delivery letters this morning before breakfast. Gee, I didn't know I was so popular! Arthur sent me some money and Bill did too. I purchased myself a new pair of blond pumps and hose and purse. Just showed myself right! Trunk hasn't arrived yet. Do hope I can get away from this place soon. Arthur Craig and I had a "round" this morning over James Leonard. They won't let him come to see me. "Good bye"! He has just got a dirty deal all around. Saw Jesse Hahn uptown "good lookin'" (and just as tough) as ever.

March 9: No trunk yet! Sent telegram to Arthur special delivery letter by Denny. I'm worried crazy. Head hurts so, am going to bed.

March 10: No trunk yet. Begins to look as if I am doomed here. Rec'd the dearest and sweetest letter from Bill. He's the sweetest boy in the world. The kids have been so mean, just driving me crazy. Rec'd Arthur's telegram but no way to get to town, no one to stay with the babies. It's a bad old rainy night, but thank goodness, it isn't cold.

March 11: Went to town to get money order. Got "Sporting News". Fellow over at Rogers Drugs told me where to go. Paid laundry, went to the Express office and inquired about my trunk. Herbert Crowder is chief "man in charge" there. Am going to bed early, have a headache.

March 12: Big snow here, trunk finally arrived. Sure is in bad shape. Got a box over at Dillards to express my linen and blankets, have my trunk partly packed. Guess I'll leave sure enough Sunday. That is if Arthur sends me the money. Have a terrible headache (as usual) These kids...Lordy!

March 13: Today is Saturday. James Leonard came in. Rec'd money order from Arthur. James Leonard kept the kids and sent my box out. I went to town, had my hair cut, and shopped some. Went home, prepared supper. Had call from Arthur E. Craig, they sure are "roarin;" because James Leonard is staying over night with me.

March 14: Sunday. Got up early, had waffles for breakfast. James Leonard helped. Then called on Mr. Craig. I had some time calling a taxi, just rushed down there and found the train was 1 hr and 40 minutes late. Arrived in Mattoon at 12:10. Ate dinner and then. The kids had had it. Met an interesting kid in the subway. Arrived in Jamesville 8 P.M. Mr. Hill was there, drove out in a snowstorm. Trunks didn't ccme. Mrs. Landrus is here. Mrs. Hill looks so bad, so does Walter. Clarence and Ruby are big. (More of Arthur's relatives) I am so tired.

NOTE TO DEAR READERS.

John Hill & Mrs. Florence Hill were Arthur's parents...Josephine's in-laws. They may not have known that Josephine had left Arthur. She probably needed a place to stay while she made her mind about what she was going to do.
Mrs. Landrus was a neighbor of the Hill family and possibly a relative. Maybe a cousin.
Mrs. Hill had diabetes and Walter Hill was her oldest son. He had Parkinson's disease and had returned

from Oklahoma where he worked as a carpenter with Arthur years before.

March 15: Kids all went to Sunday School. Mrs. Heath came over and George stopped in. Mr. Hill got my trunks. He broke 10 dozen eggs on the way that he had planned to sell. Just quiet day or quiet as it could be with these little cyclones! Rec'd Arthur's letter, also the one from Bill that he sent Friday.

March 16: Sadie and Owen (Arthur's sister and brother-in-law) came over. She gave me a crocheted centerpiece. Am afraid I'll be getting fat, I sure wade in the cream. Fixed Clarence's sweater for him. He sure is a nice kid. Ruby said he talked about me, "his Aunt Jo all the time". He sure can blush.

March 17: Mr. Hill made breakfast. He is a dandy cook too. St. Patrick's Day, well, Erin go Braugh! Mr. Hill went to Mattoon today. No word from my Bill, wish he would write.

NOTE TO DEAR READERS.

It appears that Josephine stayed with her in-laws for several weeks while she decided what she would do next. By the following entries, it seems that she did not give Bill up, as her husband, Arthur, had demanded. Again, it appears she was staying away from Arthur but using her in-laws as the excuse for her delay in returning to Oklahoma.

April 15: Arrived back in Okmulgee 10:00. Met Bill in Tulsa, came out to the house. Gibb was down, think Bill came with him.

April 16: did my washing, went for a drive. Ball season is on, little Jimmie hurt his arm but we won!

DEAR READERS: *Based on the next entries, it appears that Josephine left Arthur...**once again**...and continued her relationship with Bill. It also seems that she may have left her sick babies....with a woman named Gladys...when she was out with Bill.*

May 17: Well, up again. Everything is all over...poor lil' Billie will never be. (*Miscarriage*)

Got my trunk Saturday. Been here about six weeks. Peg was here Wednesday; same old Peg. My babies have had the chicken pox, but Gladys is so good to take them. I shouldn't really worry. This is twice I've pulled the same stunt in the last year. (*Had miscarriages*).

May 22: Went down to see my babies...Gladys had taken them visiting but came back. Arthur came over and took Gladys and me to the depot. Acted very indifferent...Mr. Pierce still having trouble.

May 23: Bill and I went out to Sunset and danced. Bill is mad at me for wearing rouge. Saw several people from Okmulgee!

DEAR READERS: This *sighting, no doubt, added fuel to the fire of the marriage falling apart*

May 24: Just fooled around in the sun - burned my shoulders all-rightee!!. Had a thrilling time with the Peoria Chiefs!... (baseball team)

May 25: Peggie came up and she and Mae had been to Bartlesville to the ball game Sunday.

May 26: Bill and I went down town to see "Ranson's Folly". Came home and then back to town, just bummed around. Rec'd letter from Lucille, she moved again. Also one from James Leonard.

May 27: Bill home all day, looking for a job. Went over to Mrs. Schrantz and then out with Bill out after. Went out to Sunset, just looked around. Jimmie playing at Muskogee.

May 28: Stayed at home all day – no mail. Bill and I went to the park, came back early. Bill's back hurt. Two girls killed at Sand Springs.

May 29: Another hot old day, 96 degrees. Went out to Sunset, had a nice time. Bill angry with me as usual. Arthur was there and also blonds from Okmulgee. Walked home.

May 30: Sunday, didn't do anything. Bill slept all day, rained and rained. Went to the show, "His People", enjoyed it immensely. And then got soaked.

May 31: Memorial Day. Bill worked... Went down to the Orpheum and enjoyed it so much. The Indian Chief sung so splendid. Peg came by this evening, went out to Sunset. Also had a flat.

June 1: Bill went to work for MacCollugh. Gibb came over and ate lunch with us. Then he and I drove to Claremore. We all went out to Sand Springs. Bill skated and his blooming skate came off. Heard some singing.

June 2: Went shopping with Mabel and Mrs. R. Seen the sweetest little dresses. Gibb came by, went for a ride and got soaked.

June 3: Mabel and I went out to Mays to have her dress fitted then drove down town to a show. Took the laundry out to the laundry woman. Bill and I called on Mr. Swartz and played "Moonlight and Roses" to my heart's content. Came back to the café, met Gladys and the other girls.

June 4: Mrs. R. & Mabel went shopping. I was alone, slept all evening. Bill mad at me. Ate alone. He & Gibb went to get a drink, hope they enjoyed it. Talked to Bernice but didn't wait for Gladys.

June 5: Went to town, purchased myself a lace dress and slip. Gibb drove me home. We went to town. Bill mad as usual. Gladys had a date. Went to the show and then home. Wish Bill would get over being mad all the time.
June 6: Sunday. Bill slept all day. So lonesome. Went over to Sunset. Lee angry because I didn't call him. Can't be bothered...I love Bill but wish he was just a little different.

***
The Diary stopped then. It picked up again in 1927….*over a year later*.

June 26: Lost another baby, April 18th...why? I can't understand and a little boy too. Seven months along and he was Bill's & mine. Operated on May 15, terrible, know what it is like to die!

DEAR READERS, *if you are keeping count, this would be 6 pregnancies with 3 living children as a result. Josephine is 25 years old. She has been pregnant for the past 8 years starting in 1919 when she was 18 years old.*

June 27: Over a year since I wrote...so much happened...came down to Okmulgee June 9th. Still here and Bill is gone again. He left today for Indianapolis with Bress..seems so lonesome. Carl took us to the train and then was over tonight telling lies. I won't believe anything he tells on Bill. Peg came by for beer.

June 28: Rec'd letter from Lucille, want to go home so bad. Nothing doing here and so lonesome. Dick came after "old 58". Nobody but my Bill, **Nobody**!

June 29: "Thinking of you, feeling kind of blue, Wondering if you're thinking of me too. Tears begin to fall, answering the Call, of Love's old golden dreams. My heart is asking for your smile. Wanting and Loving you all of the while. Wishing you were here. I'm thinking just thinking of you" I want you, Bill, want you so. Ed Farris and Mr. Phelps out for wine. Mildred came up, she & Gladys gone to swim. Carl came over, wanted me to go to Minots...**NO!** going to bed.

June 30: No letter yet. Not much of a day. Chatted with Mrs. Langwell. Jackie Jo don't feel so good, called the doctor and talked to him. Moses came out. Carl over – we had chicken sandwiches. Peg came by for some beer. She and Eva think Troy heard everything. We all looked keen, trailing out to car with beer. I love you, my darling Bill, I do, I do.

July 1: Received a letter from my Bill! He is at Indianapolis, seems so far away. Peg called, was with her all evening. She was mad at "Lefty". She got some "licker" down at the Maine. John and some guy from N.C. came out, drunk as usual. Had some good barbeque, out to Hi's.

July 2: Rec'd a letter from my Man, he is at Hamilton. I miss him so. Wrote him a letter but was so tired, I didn't get to town to mail it. Mildred & Carl came over. I was so sleepy. The boys went to the show and the twins and I slept all evening.

July 3: Sunday just another old day. The kiddies all went to Sunday school. Got the kids some fireworks. Carl took me to town, ate supper with him and then went to the show. I saw Johnny and Alice. My slip showed a mile. Sent a letter to my boy. I'm blue, blue, blue. Could hardly make it home my tummy ached so bad – walked too. Tomorrow the Grand and Glorious Fourth!

July 4: Celebrated by washing laundry. Went to town to the show tonight. Saw "Rolled Stocking" not *"sox"* as Jackie Jo says. Came back and talked to Mrs. Sell a long time. Peg & Jerry came by after some beer. Lefty staying with Mae. Peg better mind her "P's and Q's".

July 5: Went to town this evening to buy Jimmie's underwear. Rec'd a letter telling of Arthur's mother's death. She was so sweet and nice. Gladys got herself a portable record player. She's playing "Blue Skies". Rec'd letter from my homme (man), I'm missing him oodles.

July 6: Just another old hot day. Went to see "The Music Master". Saw Carl and Mrs. Beam. Came home early. Sent Mon Cherie (my love) a letter. Vera came after Pattie Jean, kept her all day.

July 7: Rec'd letter from my Bill. Sure is good about writing. Frank came over to mail letter to Lucille. Went down town to mail my letter. Carl stewed.

July 8: Mr. Barber went back to Muskogee. Clyde came by tonight, working in Henryetta, said he was talking to Harry. Rec'd my letter from Bill; think he is missing "someone" mighty bad.

July 9. Saturday and no letter. Mr. Collette came out and we went after some peanuts. Peg and Lefty came past. Washed all the kids' hair.

July 10: Seems as if this was the most blue Sunday I ever saw. Kiddies all went to Sunday school. Pattie Jean looked so sweet in the little dress I made her. Mr. B. & Gladys took me down to the show and saw "Reservation".

July 11: Today Jimmie was seven! Baked him a cake and got him a bathing suit. Got the sweetest letters from Bill. Wish.... but what's the use of wishing.

July 12: Got letters from Bill and James Leonard. Mrs. Mont for lunch and went to the show. Some guy stopped me. These men!

July 13: No letter. Made Pattie Jean a combination suit – underwear with a top and bottom that button together. Jimmie went swimming, sunburned so bad. Went to bed early.

July 14: Had a fuss with G. Rec'd a letter from Lucille and Bill. Went to show, "Heart of Salome". Came home and went to bed.

July 15: Rec'd another letter perhaps he is missing me – hope so. Just washed my face and think I'll go to bed. I love you, Bill!

Pattie Jean Hill -1927

July 16: Saturday. Rec'd card from Bill, wish he were here. Went to town with Flo and Mr. B. Came home and went to bed. These monotonous cramps!

July 17: Sunday –kiddies all went to Sunday school. Pattie Jean stayed with Vera. Working on another little dress for Pattie Jean. Arthur drove up about 1 o'clock. Took a ride with him in his Ford roadster, drove to Morris and had a flat. Gladys took Pattie Jean and Jackie Jo to Holdenville for a visit with Arthur. (Arthur is working in Holdenville) Seems so lonesome without them. Went to see "Children of Divorce".

July 18: Washed and scrubbed today and then went to the show this evening. Ronald C. "One Night of Love". It sure was a good one. He is just the kind of man women love. Gathered the clothes in, it looks like rain. I miss Bill. There is something nice about every man but there is everything nice about him. Boys have gone to church down on the corner. Jimmie got a haircut. Wonder how my babies are? Bless their sweet baby hearts. I miss them so, want to hear that "Dodo cook supper". Come back soon, Bill.

July 19: No letter, ironed this morning. Been so warm all day. Jimmie has gone on a picnic. Have been reading some old letters of Bill's. Am going to bed, Jimmie has come home.

July 20: Well, Bill came back. Just gone three weeks exactly. Called me about five – had me fooled for awhile – was so glad to see him. Mr. Barker called.

July 21: Bill and I walked over to Greenwood. Saw Mildred go in, ye Gods! Roy Scott came by and stayed.

July 22: Gladys came back with the babies. Pattie Jean hurt her finger. Was so glad to see them. Boys went to Rotary Park.

Sept 14, 1927: Rec'd letter from Lucille. Her baby was born Sunday.

***

That is the end of the diary.

Autumn, 1927

Arthur started divorce proceedings in the fall of 1927, stating that Josephine, his wife, had left him in 1925 with the three children. He made every attempt and effort to have her return but she did not. Sometime after September, 1927, Jimmie and Jackie Jo were living with him. Pattie Jean was still living with Josephine. The Judge ruled Josephine was at fault in the marriage and Arthur was awarded complete custody of all three children. Arthur was not comfortable about caring for a little girl. He decided to leave Pattie Jean with her mother. What would become of them all?

JOSEPHINE AND BILL DRAIN.

Josephine and Bill Drain moved to Tulsa, Oklahoma in the hopes of starting their new life together. Bill often got jobs as a house painter and jack-of-all-trades. His interest in making gadgets that would make work easier and more efficient continued to emerge.

Josephine was happy to have Pattie Jean to care for but she missed her little boys very much. It wasn't long before she became a mother again. This time it was a girl who was born on May 18, 1928. She was named Elizabeth Lucille Drain. She was called "Bettie" all her life. And on September 25, 1930, a little boy came into the family. He was named Billy Joe Drain.

The Drain family had originated in Ireland as **_Adrain_** from the County Rosscommon. The original family moved north to Uster to seek their fortune. Bill's father was Amos Arthur Drain – born in 1870. He moved to Oil City, Ohio and married Ada Dibble.

Their only child was **Herbert Delos Drain** who became Josephine's "Bill." No one is sure why H.D. Drain changed his first name to Bill, but he was known as Bill among his family and friends all of his life. He used H.D.

Drain as his legal and business name. He was born on August 24, 1904 in Ohio City, OH. Bill considered himself a real Irish lad. He loved the stories of the days back in Ireland. He was said to have "kissed the Blarney Stone" as he could entertain people with his wonderful personality. He also like to "tip a few" at the local tavern and sometimes he "tipped quite a few," truth be told.

The Depression period in the United States had begun in late 1929 and the worst of the period would be in 1933. This affected Josephine and Bill's family greatly. Times were very tough for the little family. Bill worked very hard at any job he could find to bring in money. Josephine continued to cook and sew and make do with what they had. She was kept so busy with the children and the daily struggles that she didn't write in her diary on a regular basis any more. She would write poems from time to time. She did continue her letter writing, especially to her sister, Lucille. They corresponded for their entire lives, sharing family information, joys and sorrows, despair, worries and plenty of love.

As the Depression continued, times got very rough. Josephine and Bill Drain took their family of five back to Illinois. They settled in Chicago where Bill hoped to find more work in the big city. It wasn't long before another baby arrived. It was May 13, 1932 and his name was Donald Michael. Just over a year later, on June 24, 1933, Thomas Delos arrived and he was followed by another daughter on May 6, 1936. She was named Mary Kathleen. The boys went by the names of Billy, Mike, and Tom. The girls were Pattie Jean, Bettie and Kathy. A huge family of 6 children. They were all healthy and happy and thrived in Chicago. Life started to improve.

The following is an article that Pattie Jean wrote in later years about her childhood.

"I remember the ice carts that came down our street every afternoon during the Depression years.
The housewives had a rectangular card with different sizes marked on each side which they placed in a window so the ice man could see it plainly and chip out a block of ice of the requested size. We lived in Chicago in an apartment on the second floor, so the ice man would have to trudge up and down two flights of stairs for a 25 cent sale.

While he was doing this, hordes of children would congregate around the ice wagon which was pulled by a plodding old horse. The bigger boys would climb into the wagon and hand out chips and small pieces of ice to the smaller kids. If there were not enough scraps to go around, the more courageous leaders would chip away at the huge block of ice.

The wagon was wood and there was straw on the floor where the ice was piled, so sometimes you had straw or a sliver of wood to crunch along with your piece of ice. This was our Dairy Queen and McDonald"s!

Many times the ice man would return before we all had a bit of ice and he would shoo us away, much as his old horse would shoo away the flies that buzzed around its head and tail. As hot and crowded as the city was, most families bought ice at least every other day, so our scattering would only be for a few minutes as the ice man would stop in front of the next house.

Being the oldest of six children, three boys and three girls, I would wait until the other bigger boys left and then I would sit on the back of the wagon and scoop up bits of ice for my brothers and sisters. Since this was during the Depression (around

1936) everyone in our neighborhood had ice boxes and garbage burner cooking stoves.

The stoves were very adaptable, as you could cook, heat your kitchen, and burn your trash all on one appliance. Most of them used coal, wood, paper, garbage or other fuel.

Ours had four burners and an opening to put in the fuel and an ash box that had to be dumped periodically. We had a little tool – a metal handle with a hook on the end like a can opener which hooked onto an indentation in the burner or fuel opening so you could put your fuel under just one or two burners if you wished.

Very little trash collected in our house in a week's time except for the bottles and cans. Food was not wrapped and rewrapped in boxes as it is today. Even our crackers and cookies were bought loose, at so much per pound and meats and fruits were not prepackaged. Meat was cut as you bought it and even lunch meat was wrapped in brown butcher paper with a tiny piece of glazed paper inside to keep it from sticking.

The grocer and butcher were nice about giving samples of their wares and many a slice of salami or chunk of cheese I enjoyed while doing the family shopping. My mother was usually busy with a baby at home so I was sent to the store to buy the food. After buying the groceries, I would have to carry them home.

More than once, I would have two bags to carry and have to walk three or four blocks each way. I usually didn't mind as it might take me one or two hours to do the shopping and I was on my own and not accountable to anyone. I enjoyed looking in the windows of all the stores in our neighborhood or learning about the new ones when we moved to a different neighborhood.

Shopping, emptying the ash box and the ice box water pan and baby-tending were my chores. I never learned to cook or clean until after I was married, as my mother would say "Pat, take the little ones to the park for the day."

The six of us would be gone from 10:00 A.M. until 4: 00 P.M. That gave my mother some peace and quiet, kept me from learning any household skills and stifled any desires I might have had to grow up and get married and have lots of children."

Written by Patricia J. Gregg 1990
    * * *

Josephine was an avid reader and that joy has passed down throughout the generations since. Josephine and Bill did continue to enjoy the movies when they had the money to attend and Josephine would often describe the movies when she wrote letters to her friends and family.

"Dear Frank **(friend of Lucille's) he was in the armed forces somewhere**....

.......I like those pictures depicting the life of some famous person. I got a lot of laughs out of Bob Hope and Bing Crosby in "Road to Morocco" too. I read "Random Harvest", all about a man or rather a soldier that was the victim of amnesia but am afraid you would be bored with it.

I read in some letters from home that Delphine's brother's son was missing. I suppose you knew old Mrs. C. was very low. She is very old. Too bad Richard isn't home to help.

I received a letter from Lucille this afternoon. She said she was planning on coming back this summer but said it depended on you, of course. She sent me some pictures and one of the new baby, with you and her. Norma (Lucille's daughter) is getting so big.

89 -

Did you hear about the shoe rationing? Won't hurt me any, but am a little worried about the kids. But one consolation is in the summer the boys can go barefoot.

***

Dear Lucille:

Here is a poem I found that you might want to use in a letter to Frank.

***

"Here, take my heart, 'twill be safe in thy keeping
While I go wandering o'er land and sea.
Smiling or sorrowing, waking or sleeping
What need I care so my heart is with thee?
It matters not where I may now be a rover
I care not how many bright eyes I see.
Should Venus herself come and ask me to love her
I'd tell her I couldn't... my heart is with thee."

This was written centuries ago by the great Irish poet Moore but could well apply to these times now.

Or perhaps you would like this.....

★★★

"I love you not only for what you are
But for what I am when I am with you.
I love you not only
For what you have made of yourself
but for what you are making of me."
★★★

Enough of this…answer soon and tell Frank to take good care of himself. All my love to you…..

Love Jo

Chicago, IL. 1942

Pattie Jean waited impatiently for the birth certificate to arrive from Oklahoma. She needed the document to get a job in the defense company. She wanted to start earning some money. She was tired of being responsible for her brothers and sisters. She never wanted to have children. They were too hard to handle. She wasn't even sure if she wanted to get married at all!

Even though she loved Papa with all her heart, she remembered how many times Mama cried herself to sleep at night because he was at the tavern. Pattie Jean wanted to enjoy the good things in life, the things she saw in the movie magazines that her friends bought. Pretty clothes and shoes and hats, having dates with handsome men, a better future and something to look forward to in her life. She wanted an exciting life like her Aunt Lucille had.

Her Mama had been sick for a while now; she had to rest during the day more and more. Fortunately Bettie was taking over most of the housework and the cooking. Bettie had usually stayed home helping Mama over the years taking care of Kathy while Pattie Jean took the boys to the park all day.

Finally, the envelope Pattie Jean had been watching for came in the mail. She eagerly opened it up and read the contents. Yes, there was Mama's name, Josephine Louise Dawson, and there was Papa's...... But… but it didn't say Herbert Delos Drain..... It said Arthur Tecumseh Hill! What? There must be a mistake! This must not be her birth certificate after all. But the birthday was correct....January 11, 1924. And it does say female. But what does number 2 of 2 births mean? She spent several days looking at the document. Finally she decided she had to ask Mama. Mama had never talked about her family or her life before Papa so Pattie Jean had to wait for just the right moment. She prepared a nice cup of hot tea and knocked on her Mama's bedroom door. Pattie Jean told Mama that the birth certificate had arrived but there was something wrong with it. It didn't have Papa's name on it.

Mama took a deep breath and said "Pattie Jean, this is something I never wanted to tell you but now I must. Papa is not your real father."

Pattie Jean gasped "But Mama, I love him and he loves me, I know he does!"

Mama smiled and said, "Of course, he loves you. He has loved you since the first time he saw you. He feels you are as much his child as the rest of our children."

"But, Mama, does that mean that Bettie, Kathy, and the boys are not my real sisters and brothers? How can that be? What happened, Mama?"

"They are just like your real brothers and sisters. I am their Mama and your Mama. But Papa is their father and he is not your real Papa." Mama replied softly. Mama started to cry. "This is too hard to talk about. Your father is Arthur Hill. I was married to him before I met Papa."

"Mama, then what does this part mean, female, 2 of 2?" Pattie Jean asked, starting to cry herself.

Mama said, "Pattie Jean, I just can't talk about it, I'm sorry. Please leave me alone now and let me rest. I'm sorry, I just can't discuss it." She turned her face to the pillow and sobbed.

Pattie Jean quietly left the room and shut the door. "What was so terrible Mama can't even tell me?" Pattie Jean thought. She looked at the birth certificate constantly. She finally decided that there must have been another baby that died at birth...a twin! Pattie Jean wondered if it was a girl or boy. Pattie Jean decided she would never ask Mama again because it upset her so much. She did not want to see her Mama cry any more. If she ever got to California, she would ask Aunt Lucille. Aunt Lucille would tell her the truth, she was sure of it.

Chicago, IL. 1943

Pattie Jean started her new job working at the defense plant. She liked the work and was occasionally asked to work nights so the timekeeper could have an extra evening off. She enjoyed dating. She had many gentlemen callers. They often went to the movies or roller skating. She liked to copy the hair styles of the movie stars, She also decided that she was too old to be called Pattie Jean. She preferred Patricia but mostly was addressed as Pat.

She had one special boyfriend who wanted to get married. Patricia felt she was too young and wasn't really sure she wanted to be married right then. The boyfriend, Bob Peltz, was in the Navy and leaving for parts unknown.

He had talked about working on a farm when he got back home. He had met her Uncle James Leonard and he really thought farm life was the way of the future. Pattie Jo wasn't sure she wanted to live in the country, away from all the movie theaters and the restaurants and shops and interesting places to go.

May 9, 1943

Dear Lucille:

Happy Mother's Day. It's raining cats and dogs here. I am alone. The kids are at the show and Bill is drunk. Been drunk since Thursday.

My morale is down to rock bottom right now. Haven't heard from Frank yet. You forgot to give me his new address. Did you send him my letter? I bet you and Norma are having a nice time in San Diego. Bob Peltz likes the Navy very much. The shots made him feel pretty bad for a few days, otherwise he is fine. He sent me two lovely pillow tops for Mother's Day, similar to the one Frank sent me. I like them, but I need pillows for them before I put them out.

I put the musical program in my scrapbook. I would like to see something like that. I went to see "Random Harvest" last night. Ronald Coleman was outstanding in his part. He is really a gentleman in every sense of the word.

I heard Eddie Cantor's program but not the rest that you spoke of.

Haven't heard from James Leonard for ages and how is Aunt Susan? I never received an answer to my letter and birthday card.

Your letter worried me. The part about the lady being operated on...but what can I do? There is no one to watch the children. Bill wasn't home three nights last week. I can't depend one bit on him for anything. I have come to the conclusion that he just doesn't give a damn.

I carry all the oil for the stove even – so I can't ask him to do anything. I do intend to see a doctor but I keep bleeding a little or all the time. I feel embarrassed going like that.

Where is Lee now? Is she still married or what? Pat is working all right. She worked nights last week to relieve the night timekeeper. She has registered at the University of Chicago for a summer course in Office Management. It's free, of course. She is entitled to a raise now but hasn't heard anything for sure. She hasn't been anywhere since Bob left on the U.S.S. Alaska,... only to work. I sent that clipping, thought you might remember him.

Kathleen was seven last Thursday. Pat gave her a little dollhouse and Bill got her a little doll. This week is Mike's birthday and the following week is Bettie's, with Bob's in-between. May is really a birthday month for us. Well, Lucille, I hope you can read this and will be looking for an answer soon.

With Love, Jo

........part of letter written to Frank...

...Lucille doesn't like California, nothing about it. The subway was opened here for a limited number of passengers only those that bought $1000 War Bonds were eligible. (I didn't ride!)
All of Pat's boyfriends are gone. I mean her school friends are scattered over America. Steve, the boy that took her to the class prom is in Kansas City training in radio work. Robert May is in Florida in the Air Corps. Bob Proctor is in Florida, Max at Camp Roberts, Russell in N. Dakota, so you can see how far away they all are.

Glad you liked the poetry, here is something more to read.

***

"My fear, my only regret
Is the thought of leaving you.
I'll brave the reign of death
That comes from a darkened sky.
But I cannot brave the thought
Of whispering Good bye".
If by chance I'm beckoned
to a heavenly land of blue
My soul may leave this earth
But my heart, I'll leave with you."

Well, Frank, I think I have told you all the news so will sign off for this time and again, let me thank you for everything. You're a grand person and I am mighty proud to have you as a friend.

Bless you and answer soon.

Jo

***

Kathleen's Trip

You could hear the clang of the train
See the bustle at the station
And Kathleen garbed in pink and blue
Was an unthought-of, big sensation.
And all the Redcaps stared
They hoped to carry the bags
that were filled with gowns for Dolly
Tho' in truth, they were only rags.
And when the train drew out
Taking her far away
We knew that many people
Would guard her night and day.
She sat on a young man's lap that trip;
When he kissed her; she gave back two
Now, you mustn't look shocked or even surprised,
For Kathleen is only two.

By Patricia Drain

DEAR READERS: Please note that Patricia is now writing poems. This need for self-expression is being carried on by the females in the families.

Time passed slowly. The brothers and sisters were growing up. Bettie was taking over more and more of the housework, cooking and laundry. Mama seemed to be aging. She was sick more often with pain in her stomach and headaches. She was too embarrassed to see the local doctor. Sometimes, her body seemed to have a mind of its own. She felt weak. She was bleeding a little every day and she felt like she wasn't clean enough. After all those pregnancies, home births, working hard around the apartment caring for her family, she was just worn out.

DEAR READERS: You will note that Josephine had at least 11 pregnancies with 8 living children. She is 42 years old.

Papa worked less regularly even though he was still employed by Sears and Roebuck. Patricia helped out with money when she could but still, there was less money coming in. And Papa spent more time at the neighborhood tavern, so he drank up quite a bit of what he did earn.

Finally Mama went to the doctor in March of 1943. She was put into the hospital for a checkup. Papa decided to send the boys to live with Mama's brother, James Leonard.

James Leonard had married. He and his wife, Vernice, lived in the country and worked on a small farm. They didn't have any children. They were trying to adopt a little boy in the area. They had plenty of farm work for the boys to do and Kathleen could help with the house and the little foster child.

Lucille invited Bettie and Kathleen to come live with her and her daughter, Norma, in California. Bettie was eager to go but Kathleen was afraid. She was only 8 years old and she wanted to see her Mama every week. She asked if California was close enough that she could visit her Mama regularly. When she was told it was very, very far away, she decided she would go to the farm with her brothers.

Pattie Jean was working hard. She had received a small raise. She still dreamed of moving out, especially to California. She was giving most of her pay to Mama to buy food and pay the rent when Papa didn't come home with enough money. With the other children now living in California and on the farm with James Leonard; they were getting by. Aunt Lucille wrote to Mama every week and talked about how beautiful it was there. Lucille had learned to love her new location especially having Bettie there to keep Norma company. It was like having two daughters and Aunt Lucille loved them both. It was warm and sunny and everything sounded so wonderful.

Mama said they couldn't afford to move to California. Besides, Mama wouldn't leave her children, even if they were still living with Uncle James Leonard and his wife. The kids said Vernice was such a good cook that they nicknamed her Aunt Cookie and she went by that name for the rest of her life. But what the children didn't tell anyone was that their lives had changed. They were being abused on a regular basis. Uncle James Leonard had a very dark side to his personality and all of the children, including Bettie and Pattie Jean had been victims. Bettie had taken the offer from Aunt Lucille to get away from him. She had moved to California. Pattie Jean was now working and had changed her name to Patricia. She didn't have much time to visit the farm. When she wasn't at work, she was trying to help her mother at home. But the other siblings, three boys and a little girl were trapped. In those days, children didn't tell what was really happening…
***

Pattie Jean and Josephine - 1942

One day, Patricia decided to treat her Mama with a special gift. She was going to stop at the Fannie May Candy Store and buy her a piece of chocolate with the pretty little paper wrapper and have it put in a Fannie May Candy Store bag. If there was one thing Patricia knew about her mother it was that Josephine enjoyed chocolate.

She waited until payday and then walked to the candy store. It was late, nearly 6:00 P.M. As she was walking to the front door, she bumped into a young man who was also trying to enter. Patricia stopped quickly, smiled and said, "I'm sorry, I wasn't looking. I hope I didn't step on your foot."

The young man looked at her and with a smile, he replied, "No, I'm fine. Please let me get the door for you."

"Oh, thank you." Patricia said, feeling a blush all over her face. She was so embarrassed. "Thank Goodness", she said to herself that she had a fresh white blouse on today and her best black skirt. She had even tied a white ribbon in her hair because this was a special purchase. She wanted to look grown-up and act as if she knew what she was doing.

As she entered the Fannie May Candy Store, she stopped to look at the white wicker baskets of candy. Each white basket had a different pastel color of ribbon and netting tied to the handle. Every color and shape of candy she could imagine was there. The store smelled so good, she wanted to stay there forever. Finally she saw a chocolate fudge piece that looked so beautiful she couldn't believe it was really candy.

As the clerk approached her, Patricia said softly, "How much is that piece, please?"

The clerk was dressed in a sparkling white uniform with a white ruffled apron. She was a sweet faced, soft spoken woman. She said, "Why, it is 50 cents, dear."

"Oh My", Patricia replied, "I don't have enough for that piece. It was going to be a surprise for my Mama. She has not been feeling well for a long time and I wanted to cheer her up. I guess I will have to save more money and come back later."

She turned away and started towards the door.

"Wait, please!" It was the young man she had bumped into at the door. He turned to the clerk and said, "Mother, can we afford to buy that piece of candy for this young lady's mother?"

Smiling, the clerk said, "Of course, we can. Every mother would like to get a piece of candy from a beautiful daughter like this one."

With that, she scooped up the candy, wrapped it in tissue and put it in an especially tiny little Fannie May bag and tied it up with a ribbon, just like the pastel ribbons on the candy baskets in the display area. She handed the bag to her son, who turned to Patricia.

"I hope your Mama likes the candy." My name is Donald Vietinghoff and this is my mother, Leonette. I came to walk Mother home tonight. May we walk you home as well? It is getting very dark outside."

Patricia stuttered, "Oh, I don't know if that is proper. And I just live a few blocks from here. "

Leonette said to Patricia. "Please, dear, let us walk you home. We live on Clark Street. and I'm sure you don't live much farther. You work in the neighborhood, don't you? I think I have seen you pass by a few times. What's your name?"

Patricia smiled and said, "Yes, I do work nearby. My name is Pattie Jean… Oh; I mean...Patricia Drain and it would be very nice to walk with you."

Patricia hoped they didn't notice her hesitation in saying her name; she thought Patricia sounded much more grown up than Pattie Jean.

Several weeks went by and Patricia continued to dream of California. She didn't see how she ever would be able to afford to go there, even just visit Aunt Lucille. She knew Mama was getting worse. She seldom felt up to doing anything. When Papa would invite Mama out for a movie, she would not go. She just had no strength any more. She was still interested in getting letters and keeping in touch with the children out at the farm but that was all that she seemed to care about now.

Patricia spent more time alone at home. She tried her hand at writing poems and stories. She didn't show them to anyone....it was her way of dealing with feeling so sad.

**

Graduation

I shall leave behind a million pleasant things...
Things I can never recapture.
Time between school periods.
Eating peanuts and potato chips.
Chatter over a Coke.
Laughs and jokes that weren't funny.
School play rehearsals again and again.
Moments of breathless excitement before the curtain rises.
Now they are all behind.
But this isn't time for sadness...
This should be some of the best hours of my life.
I'm growing up....I'm graduating...
No long just a high school girl...
No longer a child...almost a woman now.
Ahead lies...marriage or a career?
Happiness or sorrow?
Adventure and excitement?
Or just simply living.
I wish I knew.

***
GIVE ME A KISS

Give me a kiss, a kiss just meant for me
Give me a kiss that will last an eternity
I realize that the love in your eyes isn't just for me.
But my heart simply won't agree.
So give me a kiss and I vow that I will never forget
Memories of days when we two were happy...yet
I always knew you'd never be true
And it would come to this.
But darling, before you go, give me a kiss.

Written by Patricia Drain – 1942
***

THE VIETINGHOFF FAMILY HISTORY.

The Vietinghoffs can be traced back to Ferdinand Albert Friedrich von Vietinghoff (born 1-15-1819) in Ludwigsburg, Germany. He married Adrigunde E. von Starker in Germany. She was born there on 10-11-1839. They immigrated to the United States in 1857 and lived in Wilmington, IL. The von Vietinghoffs stopped using the **_"von"_** which means "from a family of nobility" when they came to America.

One of their sons was Oscar Arthur Vietinghoff. He was born on 8-19-1859 and married May Carpenter in Spring Valley, IL. She was also born in 1859. One of their children was **Arthur Louis Vietinghoff**. His birth date was 12-20-1899. He married **Leonette L. Morris** in 1916. Her birth date was 10-10-1899. They had 9 living children. Arthur Lewis born on 7/1/1917; Marjorie Helen on 11-23-1918, Catherine Jean on 1/19/1922, **Donald Francis Vietinghoff** on 8/4/1923, William Lloyd on 3/23/1926, Virginia Druzilla on 10/24/1927, twin sons Robert Morris on 12/24/1929 and Leo Morris on 12/25/1929 and Donna Mae on 5/18/1931.

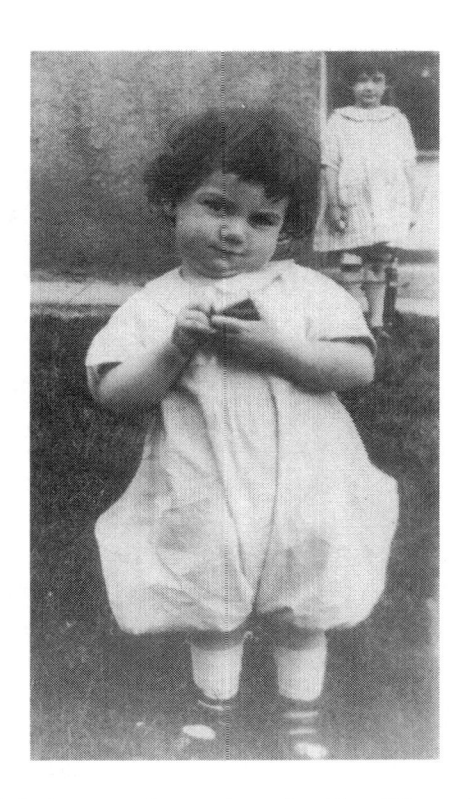

<u>Donald Francis Vietinghoff - 1926</u>

The Chicago years...1942

    Patricia would stop by to talk to Leonette at the Fanny Mae Candy Store from time to time. They formed a wonderful friendship. Leonette became like a mother to Patricia. They were both very fond of each other.

    Occasionally, Donald would stop at the store to walk his mother home and he would talk to Patricia. He was so handsome, almost like a movie star in her eyes. He had dark black curly hair and a dimple. He was quite a gentleman and dressed very nicely. He worked for a small lithograph printing company. He lived with his mother and brothers and sister in an third floor apartment on Clark Street. near Patricia's home with her parents.

Finally he asked Patricia if she would like to see a movie with him one evening.

"Of course." she said "Yes, I would love to." Inside, she was jumping up and down, "Oh Yes,…Yes…Yes!"

They did go out a few times and became more and more interested in each other. They enjoyed talking about books and music and art. Patricia already loved his mother and wanted to meet his brothers and sisters…all of them.

He told her that his father, Arthur, had been a bread salesman in Illinois. When Donald was a young boy, he recalled that Arthur would take him along on Saturdays as he ran his route and collected the money. Donald remembered that his father always stopped at a particular house and stayed inside for a long time. Eventually Donald realized his father was having an affair with the woman in the house. Donald was very upset that his mother was being betrayed. He vowed when he graduated from high school that he would leave home. He did graduate as scheduled and he did move to Chicago to live with a relative there.

Donald's brothers, Arthur Jr. and William and a sister, Marge, who was a nurse, had already left home. Catherine and Virginia, two of his other sisters, had married and lived in Minonk, IL. This was near the area where the entire family had lived for years. After Donald left home, their father decided to move the rest of the family to Chicago some months later. Once he had moved them to Chicago, into the apartment, Arthur left them all with no explanation. Arthur Sr. filed for divorce and never returned. They couldn't afford to move back to their former home town.

Donald had 8 brothers and sisters in all. Donald moved in with his mother, Leonette, and the twins Leo and Robert, and little sister Donna. They were living in the 3 bedroom, 3rd floor walk up apartment.

It was a necessity for Leonette to find a way to provide for the rest of her family. She got her first job with Fannie May Candy Store. Over the years, the children helped out as they grew old enough to work. The twins decided to join the Navy. Donald had tried to enlist but had been turned down because of his eyesight. But he was working and could help with the expenses. Donna was still in high school.

Patricia finally got to meet all of the family that still lived in the area. Donald also took her to Minonk, IL. to meet his sisters and brothers-in-law. She had an instant liking for Virginia and Catherine. She felt like they were sisters. The girls were very much like Leonette, their mother. They were loving and sweet and happy to meet her. She felt very accepted and loved by all the Vietinghoff family.

Patricia continued to write letters to Bob Peltz who was in the Navy. She told him that she felt she had changed since he had left home. She felt more grownup, perhaps due to her mother's illness. She told him about her job and the fact that her mother needed her to help with the finances. She felt a big responsibility towards her family. She had thought of moving to California in the hopes of seeing Bob and a possibility of marriage. But now she didn't feel she could leave her family and she wasn't sure she was still in love with Bob. She asked him if they could remain "friends" and still correspond. Patricia didn't hear anything from Bob in response. She thought she had ruined any chance of a relationship or even a friendship.

Donald's sister Catherine was living in Minonk. Her husband, Russell and his brother, Emerson, and the men's father, Jesse James Bradbury, managed a drive-in restaurant. Later they started a small grocery store. Russell joined the Navy during WWII for a short period of time. He was being trained as an underwater welder. However, his sinuses became infected and he got a medical discharge and returned home. He really didn't have an interest in working in the grocery store. After Jesse James passed away, the brothers' mother continued to live in the house next to the store. Minonk was a very small town and everyone was well known in the area. Emerson decided to carry on the family grocery business.

Virginia had been married for a few years to a traveling salesman. Unfortunately, although he was a good provider, she discovered that he had another woman on the side and so she divorced him.

Coincidentally, this is the same situation that her father, Arthur, had been in. He also had been a salesman, had a woman on the side, and eventually filed for divorce from Leonette. In fact, he was so bold about it that he had taken Donald along on some of his visits to the woman's home when Donald was a child. It wasn't until years later that Donald realized that this same woman was the reason that his father had walked out on the family after he moved them away to Chicago. It was a behavior that stayed in Donald's mind for many years.

Virginia was acquainted with the Bradbury family because her sister, Catherine, had married Russell Bradbury. She and Emerson (Russell's brother) eventually got married. **Two sisters from the Vietinghoff family married two brothers from the Bradbury family. Double cousins for all the children they might have!** Emerson really enjoyed working in the grocery store every day and was well respected in the little town. They built a house across the street from the store with a white picket fence. It was a perfect little house. They were very happy with their life. But there were no babies in spite of their desire to start their own family.

Catherine and Russell had gotten married earlier then they had originally planned. Catherine had gotten pregnant soon after high school graduation. Her father, Arthur, threw her out of the house and she married Russell in Feb. 1940. She had a stillborn baby as a result of her first pregnancy. This was followed by a second pregnancy which resulted in a son who only lived for one day. Two sad losses within the first three years of marriage. Russell had faithfully worked in the grocery store but didn't like being tied down to an inside job. He wanted to work outside and was looking for more exciting employment. Russell often talked about moving to California to find a better life.

Patricia was so envious of the two sisters. She wasn't interested in the marriage part or having children to take care of but the idea of starting a new life somewhere else was so intriging. She especially wished she could move to California or at least visit the state. She longed to see her Aunt Lucille, her cousin Norma, and her sister, Bettie. Perhaps Aunt Lucille could explain about the "twin" on her birth certificate and she would know the story at last.

Donald and Patricia had a very long talk one day. They both wanted to go to California. The only way they could afford it was to go with Russell and Catherine. It would help because there would be another man to help drive for longer periods of time. They could share motel rooms and have more money to pool together. The only way that Donald and Patricia could go, however, was to be married. Their families would not approve of them traveling together even with Russell and Catherine. It would not be proper to go as two single people. The neighborhood would talk and Patricia's reputation would be ruined forever.

In the meantime, Josephine had become ill again and was admitted to the hospital. She told Patricia that she had a visit one night in the hospital from her mother, Alice. Alice told her that if she didn't get well enough to leave the hospital by the next day, Alice was coming to get her and would "take her home." Considering that Alice had been dead for over twenty years, this gave Josephine the incentive to get out of the hospital room and back home quickly, even though she still didn't feel well.

Even though Donald and Patricia were not sure they were ready to marry, they decided they should take full advantage of the opportunity.

They got married on Feb 3, 1943 and left on their honeymoon with Catherine and her husband, Russell. They set out for California. They were hopeful for a good outcome on this new phase of their lives.

February, 1944

Both the couples enjoyed their trip to California. All of them wanted to stay but the money was running out. They didn't find any employment in the few days they were in California either.

They all decided that it would be best to return to their home state and families. Catherine and Russell went back home. Donald and Patricia went back to Chicago and found a small apartment for themselves.

The newly-married couple often visited Kathleen and the boys at the farm with Uncle James Leonard and Aunt Cookie. The farm was a relaxing place, filled with fresh air, puppies and kittens, and plenty of good home cooked food. Patricia loved to see her brothers and sister. Donald enjoyed the country life on the farm on an occasional weekend too. They took photos and brought back stories for Josephine. She felt more comfortable about the continued separation from her children.

Patricia finally got a letter from her previous boyfriend, Bob Peltz. It was sent to her in care of Uncle James Leonard at the farm in Margengo, IL.
***

July 10, 1944 from the U.S. Navy

Dear Pat:
Received two more letters from you today and it looks like I'll be able to depend on you from now on. Yes, it also seems that you've learned the meaning of mail. But you are going to have to be a little more patient than you have been so far as my mail is concerned. One of the many reasons is because it may be a long time before it leaves the ship, however, when you do get it; there will be several of them.

In my first letter I advised you to go to Norma and Lucille in California but now I take that back. This, due to two reasons, I'd like you to learn to be used to the farm life because there you'll find real happiness. The other is that it would be nice if you were to come to the West Coast but I'd better not advise it.

Pat, why do things have to work

out like this? It just doesn't seem right. The old Bob you used to know isn't there any more. I have done a lot of changing. The things I used to do don't interest me any more and life isn't as it used to be. Take my last leave; I wasn't back four days before I had the urge to move on to new places. It's been that way for the past year now. It don't make me feel bad when we "up anchor" and leave for distant ports. I'm actually glad. After this mess is over and I'm OK; maybe that will pass. Who knows, I don't!

It's just like I said - as friends we'd never last without going deeper sooner or later... and it would be sooner. I well remember my promise to always be a friend but I had no idea that it would come so soon. I don't want you to take that wrong. I fully realize that was what I meant when I promised. I was very sincere when I said that but now I see just how it was meant and what was in back of it.

I love you, Pat, *no...it's true* - always has and always will be true. I have never yet met a girl that can measure up to your qualifications. Nor have I thought that I did. I have met some really swell girls since we split up but none like you. They were just girls that a fellow could pick up and drop at the right times. It all adds up to this (with no beating around the bush), I have very little time to straighten things out and want to know just where I stand. Are you writing in the hopes that I'd forgive and forget? Would you like to take that trip you mentioned as we had planned when we came off the last one? No beating around the bush, Pat, I want facts and nothing but. My time is limited and I believe you know how! I won't back down on anything but will admit I've been hoping to hear from you for a long time.

There is one question I would like to have answered if you can remember. It's been sort of bothering me ever since it happened. Remember the last time I seen you? (I ask, please for an answer to this.) Were you or were you not still in love with me then or was it a case of not being sure???? You claim to be grown up now so you must be sure of your stance so let's have all the answers straight from the shoulder.

I hope this reaches you soon because that it means a lot – that is for "too sure". Give my regards to James Leonard and Cookie and tell him I hope to be making that trip.

Good night for now and write soon.

Love Bob

DEAR READERS: **I think it is obvious that Patricia had not written to Bob to tell him she had married. And whether she ever did give him the news is unknown. It might have been the time it took for letters to go to his ship and back to the United States that caused a delay. What I do know is that she kept this letter her whole life...still in the original envelope, tucked away in the diary her mother wrote. How different might her life have been if she had contacted Bob and they had been together?**

Catherine and Patricia were keeping up their correspondence. One day Patricia got a letter announcing that Russell and Catherine were expecting a bundle of joy in November, 1944. Catherine described her symptoms. That is when Patricia realized she might be pregnant as well. And sure enough, Donald and Patricia's baby was expected in December, 1944. Both women were very excited because their babies would not only be cousins but would be born nearly at the same time. Both men were very excited too because they would be fathers at last. These would be the first grandbabies in the family as well so everyone was looking forward to the births.

The pregnancy went well and every day Patricia noticed her body was changing. She asked Donald to take several pictures of her throughout the months of waiting. They were both so thrilled and proud.

On November 13, 1944, Russell and Catherine welcomed their first child, a girl, named Pamela Jean. Her middle name was the same as Catherine's. Catherine had read a book many years ago. The heroine was named Pamela which she thought was perfect for her first daughter.

On December 16, 1944, Donald and Patricia welcomed their daughter, Terri Jeanne...and they entered into a new chapter of their lives. Patricia had once read a movie magazine with the name Terri in it and decided it was the name she wanted for her first child. Coincidentally, Patricia's middle name was Jean also. She loved everything about the country of France so she decided to change the spelling to Jeanne for her daughter so it was a bit unusual and more "sophisticated." Catherine and Patricia always felt a special connection that they shared the same middle name as did their first-born daughters.

The two cousins, Pam and Terri, remained close all of their lives.

Terri and Pam   1946

Josephine and Donald - 1944

A few weeks later, on January 12, 1945, Mama passed away. Patricia's 21st birthday had been the day before. It was a very sad way to remember the special occasion of turning 21. Mama had only a little time with baby Terri Jeanne. Patricia was sad that Terri's maternal grandmother would not be a part of Terri's life as she grew up.

Patricia felt lost without Mama in her daily life. There were so many questions about keeping house, cooking and cleaning, and taking care of a little baby that she wanted to ask but

Mama wasn't there anymore. She turned to Leonette for comfort and guidance.

Papa was lost in his sorrow. He spent more time drinking his grief away. He spent time with Patricia and his new granddaughter. Finally, he was encouraged to start working on some bigger inventions with another man who helped finance some of the projects. The new activities seemed to help him move on.

Donald and Patricia enjoyed their apartment and their daughter. They took several pictures of her as she grew from a baby to a toddler. They managed quite well on Donald's pay. Life was good. They were proud to be keeping up on their obligations. They felt responsible and pleased with their lives.

Although Terri Jeanne was very tiny and very young, she did remember one time when Daddy spanked her. Daddy had a new radio that he was very proud to own. He had just turned it on and set the volume. Terri Jeanne had watched him and wanted to touch the knobs. She turned the volume knob and the radio got VERY LOUD.

Daddy turned it down again and said, "No, Terri." Terri Jeanne was having fun and so she twisted the knob even more. Daddy turned it down again and said firmly. "No No, Terri!" Of course, Terri Jeanne turned the knob once again and to her surprise, all of a sudden, she was lying across Daddy's knee and he spanked her two times on her diapered bottom. Terri remembered that for the rest of her life.

Now that Patricia was a young mother, once again she found her idle thoughts turning back to her teen years, especially when she got her birth certificate. Ever since the death of her mother, Josephine, in January of 1945, Patricia was even more eager to learn about her birth father. Even though Bill Drain, her stepfather, loved her as much as his other children, Patricia felt alone. Something was still missing and she wanted to know what had happened so long ago.

She was sure if she could talk to Aunt Lucille in California, the truth would come out. She had so many unanswered questions and she needed to find out the truth. She knew her Papa wouldn't tell her, even if he hadn't been drinking. He still got upset when she talked about Mama to him.

Coincidentally, Bill Drain decided to take a trip to California in 1947. He offered to take Patricia and Terri Jeanne along. The intention was to visit with Aunt Lucille and her daughter, Norma (who was just a few years younger than Patricia) and see Bettie, Patricia's sister, who had been living with Aunt Lucille for a few years. So off went the little group making their way to California.

Patricia did have that conversation with her Aunt Lucille. She was told that her mother had been married before, fell in love with Bill, and after a few years was divorced by Arthur T. Hill. She was told she had a twin brother and an older brother. Aunt Lucille encouraged Patricia to try to locate her original family in Oklahoma. Patricia believed she couldn't discuss her longing to find her birth father with Bill. She loved Bill very much and would never want to hurt him. She decided to send a letter to her birth father at his original address in the hopes that the Post Office could forward the letter to him. Aunt Lucille was sure that the Hills still lived in the same area in Oklahoma. Patricia sent the letter and wondered what the outcome might be.

A few weeks after she was back home in Chicago, the letter she had written with such care and so much hope and some dreams, was returned. The outside of the envelope was marked with all kinds of forwarding addresses but the messages that were written on the envelope broke her heart. The messages said *"Don't write here again, we don't want to hear from you." "Let us alone, you are not part of this family."* Patricia felt ashamed and even worse, rejected and alone. She couldn't understand why her father would not want to hear from her and to know what had happened to his only daughter.

In the autumn of 1947, Patricia realized that she had not been feeling well for several weeks. At first she thought she was just sad about the rejection of her birth father but she also noticed other symptoms that seemed familiar.

Soon the doctor confirmed that baby #2 was on the way. This was going to make money tight for the young family, not to mention the apartment was going to be too small. The young couple had purchased a baby buggy for Terri Jeanne when she was just a few months old and they were still paying on it every month. The buggy was very well-constructed and was big enough that Patricia could put the groceries in the buggy and still have plenty of room for Terri. As Terri got older and could sit up, there was even more room for groceries. Now they were worried about keeping up the payments on the buggy.

But it would be even more of a necessity with a second child. How could Patricia manage two small children and going to the grocery store or the park without the buggy?

Terri   1945

Leonette had only her last child, Donna, living at home. Donna was 14 years old and going to high school. The twins, Robert and Leo, had both joined the Navy and did not get home very often. A discussion and an agreement were reached that Donald and his little family would move to Clark Street to the 3rd floor apartment. This would help both families with money. Donald and Patricia could pay off the baby buggy. Patricia would have some help with the children. She could learn about cooking and cleaning from Leonette. She was especially happy to be with Leonette. Things seemed to be settling into the perfect pattern and plan once again.

Donna was not very happy with the arrangement and made sure everyone promised that Terri Jeanne would be kept out of Donna's bedroom. She also wasn't happy because she would have to share her room with Leonette once the 2nd child arrived. The bedrooms would be divided up with the front bedroom for Leonette and Donna, the second bedroom for Donald and Patricia and the new baby and the tiny back bedroom would be for Terri Jeanne. They bought a set of bunk beds so Terri could get used to sleeping in the bedroom alone. Eventually they would put the new baby in the back bedroom also. Since Donald still worked nights, the middle bedroom was quiet and dark so he could sleep without much trouble. Patricia tried to keep Terri Jeanne in the living room at the front of the apartment or on the back porch during the day. She also planned to take the children to Lincoln Park as often as possible. It would be like she was back home again as a child, taking children out for most of the day to stay out of the way at home.

On March 18, 1948, Terri Jeanne, just over 3 years old, was told that Mommy & Daddy would be bringing home a present for her! She had missed Mommy, who had been gone a couple of days. She was excited because Mommy would be coming home. It seemed like she had been gone for a very, very long time. She climbed up on the dining room chair and waited and waited. Finally the front door opened and in came Daddy and Mommy with a big bundle.

The bundle was making noises and Terri Jeanne watched carefully as the blanket was opened up. Inside was a baby girl, with dark fuzz on her head. She was crying. Her name was Virginia Lee. She was named for Donald's sister and her middle name was for Grandma, Leonette. Baby Virginia was to be called Ginny. She resembled her aunt Virginia in her looks and in her mannerisms. Terri Jeanne looked at her sister for a few minutes and then got off the chair and went to play with her doll. She didn't think that crying baby was much of a present!

As Ginny grew; Terri eventually got used to her sister and they started to play together. They would sit side by side at the kitchen table for all their meals. They shared some toys and enjoyed the attention of both Mommy, Daddy, and Grandma. And sometimes Aunt Donna too!

In February of 1950, Donald and Patricia brought another surprise home for Terri Jeanne and Ginny. Terri stood on the dining room chair and watched another blanket being opened up. Yes, it was another baby! Terri was pleased to see a beautiful baby girl with Daddy's dimple and his dark hair. Her name was Bonnie Jo. Her middle name was Jo for her maternal grandmother, Josephine.

Now the growing family had three little girls under the age of 7. The apartment was filling up, the kitchen table was stretched. There were 3 generations living there in one place.

Life continued to move along well in the 3rd story apartment on N. Clark Street, Chicago, Il. There was a nice back porch off the kitchen. The third floor apartment was high enough for a breeze to flow through. There was a stairway on the left side of the back porch which had a locked gate. The children could play outside on the porch and be in a protected area and could be seen from the kitchen door or window. The yard three floors below was mostly dirt. Some of the tenants grew vegetables to supplement their meals. The children only went down to the backyard when there was a family member with them. Walking 3 children up and down three flights of stairs was not the easiest way to spend the day.

Leonette was a wonderful cook. She prepared most of the meals and almost everything was made from scratch. She made the best cornstarch pudding.

Grandma's Corn Starch Pudding
1 c. sugar
3 rounded Tbs. cornstarch
2-1/2 c. milk
dash of salt
1 Tsp vanilla.

Mix sugar and cornstarch. Add milk, salt and vanilla. Cook until thickened...do not let it scorch. Serve hot or cold.

Donna also liked to cook. She made an unbelievably delicious banana Boston cream pie.

Banana Boston cream pie

Cake: 1-1/4 c. flour
    ¾ c. sugar
    2 Tsps baking powder
    ¼ Tsp salt
    2/3 c. milk
    ¼ c. shortening
    1 Tsp vanilla
    1 egg
Filling: ½ c. sugar
    3 Tbs flour
    1/8 Tsp salt
    1-1/4 c. milk
    1 egg, slightly beaten
    1 Tsp butter
    1 Tsp vanilla
    2 bananas, cut to ¼ thick slices
Glaze: 1 ounce unsweetened chocolate
    2 Tbs butter
    1 c powdered sugar
    1 dash salt
    ¼ Tsp vanilla
    2 or 3 Tbs milk

To prepare cake. Grease 9" round pan. Put waxed paper in bottom of pan and grease again. Blend cake ingredients and beat 2 minutes until moist. Bake in 350 degree oven for 20-30 minutes. Cool 5 minutes and invert. Cut cake horizontally into 2 slices. Cool.

Prepare filling:
Put sugar, flour, salt and milk into sauce pan. Stir completely until all

ingredients dissolve. Cook until it boils for 1 minute with continuous stirring. Carefully and slowly mix ¼ cup of hot mixture with raw egg and then pour egg mixture slowly into hot mixture. Cook and stir until bubbly. Stir in butter and vanilla, let cool and stir again. Put half of filling on bottom cake. Layer bananas on top. Cover bananas with remainder of filling.

Prepare glaze in small sauce pan. Melt chocolate and butter on low heat. Remove from heat and stir in sugar, milk, vanilla and salt. Put top layer on cake, pour glaze over top and let it run down the sides.
Refrigerate.

Mmmmmm......, the memories of those smells and tastes linger on to this day. It never lasted very long in that household either.

For breakfast, the children often ate cereal out of the box. There were little comic books like comic strips at the bottom of the box. The girls' second favorite treat was Cracker Jack because it always had a prize inside the box too.

The apartment was called a "shotgun" apartment because if you stood in the kitchen and shot a gun, the shot would go straight through to the living room. There were three rooms. One was off the kitchen in the back of the apartment, one was off the living room in the front of the apartment, and the other in the middle of the apartment. That middle bedroom was across from the bathroom where the hall had a built-in cabinet for storage and the telephone sat on the counter.

Between the hall and the living room was the dining room which had a build-in buffet. The front door was on one side of that room. On another wall was a bookcase filled with Storybook Dolls. These were small Madame Alexander dolls, dressed as a story heroines like Cinderella. They came in a cardboard box which looked like the background of the story they represented. According to Donna, children were NOT ALLOWED to touch them but they could be looked at every day. The dolls belonged to Aunt Donna and she did not want to share them!

1947 - Donna, twin Bob, Donald, twin Leo (back row)
Leonette, Patricia and Terri (front row) seated at the dining room table in front of the built-in buffet.

From the dining room, you would enter the living room with two big windows. You could see a private Catholic girls' school across the street. It was surrounded by a high brick wall all the way around the block. Terri liked to look out the windows across to the school. Sometimes, she saw the girls swinging or playing games in the yard.

One Christmas, Terri had walked into the living room. Just as she was about to sit on the couch, the white flocked Christmas tree, which seemed to touch the ceiling, fell over. Terri tried to get out of the way but the tree top hit her. She screamed and everyone rushed in to see what was wrong. The tree, being white flocking was fine, only a few ornaments broke and Terri was not injured. Another memory that has been retained to this day.

It wasn't long before Terri started kindergarten. She was walked to and from school every day. When she walked around the corner of the apartment building, she always passed a newspaper stand on the left, filled with all kinds of newspapers and magazines. But she was especially interested in the man who sat on the right side of the sidewalk. He had pencils in a cup and he was blind. Sometimes, Mommy would give Terri a few pennies to drop into the cup. The blind man always said "Thank you, Little Miss Blue Eyes." Terri could not figure out how the blind man knew she had blue eyes. And every time she passed him, he would always say "Good morning, Little Miss Blue Eyes." even if she didn't speak.

Terri and her sister, Ginny, slept in the bedroom by the kitchen in a set of bunk beds. Patricia and Donald slept in the bedroom by the bathroom. The baby, Bonnie, was still in her crib in their bedroom. Leonette and Donna slept in the bedroom by the living room in the front of the apartment.

Terri was a bit shy when she first started kindergarten but soon she learned to enjoy school and playing with other children her own age. One afternoon, one of her little friends asked her to come to his house to play after school. He only lived about a block away and so off the two children went to play. After an hour or so, his mother asked Terri where she lived and was very surprised to learn that Terri had not told her mother where she was going. Fortunately, Terri had learned her address and phone number the summer before school started. The little boy's mother quickly called Patricia and let her know her daughter was safe and what the children had done.

Terri knew her phone number by heart. She had listened to her mother say it so many times when using the phone. The telephone was on the built-in cabinet in the hallway.

It was a big black phone but this one didn't have to be cranked. When her mother picked it up, this is what she said. "My number is W as in Washington, E as in Edward, L as in Larry, another L as in Larry, I as in Iodine, N as in Never, G as in George, T as in Tom, O as in Orange ,and N as in Never. Wellington 5-4680. Then she told the operator what number she was calling.

Terri's address was 3814 Clark Street, Chicago. Il. **That is where Terri went to bed that night without any supper.** She slept in the top bunk in the bedroom next to the kitchen. She could see the sun as it went down and hear the conversation and smell the good dinner she missed that night. And she never went anywhere after school without her mother's permission from that day on!

Life continued well. Donald took up a new hobby of photographing his children. He didn't see them as much as he would have liked because he was still working nights. Often, after work at night, he would go to a restaurant in Logan's Square for breakfast. He enjoyed the meal and had some quiet time to himself before he went home to three little girls. He made some friends at the restaurant. Since Terri was the oldest, Donald occasionally took her for a few hours to the park and even to the restaurant in Logan's Square. He had gotten into the habit of talking about his oldest daughter to one of the hostesses because she had a daughter just a couple of years older than Terri. She helped Donald understand how little girls behaved and what they enjoyed doing. He thought it would make him a better father to all of his girls.

Time continued to march on. Donald was now working days as a salesman. He seemed to spend more time away from home. Living in an apartment full of all females including three little girls under the age of 7, a teenager and two grown women was probably a lot for him to take on a daily basis.

Patricia often took the girls to Lincoln Park for a picnic and to allow them to run and climb and play. It reminded her of her childhood and the many hours she spent keeping her brothers entertained. In a way it was similar because having the girls out for the afternoon allowed Leonette and Donna to have a break. It seemed like a good arrangement for everyone living in the apartment.

listening to music. Even though she came from a long line of writers and poets, she didn't take the time putting her thoughts into written words. She wasn't sure just what was wrong in the marriage but she knew there was trouble.

She kept trying to figure out what she could do to fix it. She felt very vulnerable. Her mother was gone, her stepfather, Bill, was planning a marriage which would begin a new life for him. Her sisters were not close enough to spend time with on a regular basis. Even her sisters-in law were not close by and besides, Donald was their brother so how could Patricia complain to them?

Papa had patented more inventions. He was doing better financially than he had ever imagined. Patricia didn't want to burden Bill with her problems when he was living the life he had always dreamed he would have. Her brothers and sisters were grown and scattered all over the country busily making their own hopes and dreams come true. She didn't feel that she had anyone she could confide in. She did talk to in one sister-in-law, who was married to one of Donald's twin brothers, about her worries. Shortly after that, the sister-in-law was diagnosed with polio and then found out she was pregnant as well. The sister-in-law was in a whirlwind of medical treatment and concern that the polio would cause her to have permanent disabilities and even worse, what would it do to the pregnancy? Patricia did not think she could burden anyone with her own concerns and as usual, kept her problems to herself.

Leonette Vietinghoff - 1952

Donald and Patricia - 1952

She wrote to Aunt Lucille asking for advice. Aunt Lucille suggested that Patricia try again to contact her birth father. Maybe she could visit Oklahoma. Patricia fantasized about moving to Oklahoma and spending time with her father and her twin and her older brother. She thought it would be a wonderful way to get to know the family she had lost at such a young age. Patricia called the Oklahoma telephone assistance operator and easily got the very important phone number. Patricia finally got her nerve up and made the call. The phone rang and then someone answered. Patricia explained that her mother had been Josephine and her birth certificate said Arthur T. Hill was her father. Before she could say another word, the woman on the other end of the phone interrupted her and told her that they had no desire to talk to her. She was not to call the home again. They didn't want to hear from her and she was not welcome in the family. With that, the phone was slammed down and the call was disconnected.

Patricia now felt that she was truly alone. Her birth father didn't want her and her mother was dead. Her stepfather was busy making arrangements to move to California at the insistence of his new wife. Her marriage was falling apart. She had three little girls to raise. She believed, if the marriage ended, she would also lose the love and companionship of her sisters-in-law and brothers-in-law and most of all, she would lose Leonette. She was full of despair. What was she going to do? Her own step-brothers and sisters were not around. They were living their own lives in other places now.

Leonette was quite upset about the problems. She talked to her son several times and told him she didn't want him to abandon his family like his own father had done. She reminded

Patricia – 1953

him that Patricia had no job and no experience as a working mother. She also reminded him how tough it had been on their family when Leonette had to work outside the home. Donald did understand and respected his mother's point of view. However, he just wasn't satisfied with his life as it was. He was sure things could be better, for everyone involved, if the marriage was dissolved and they moved on.

Patricia corresponded often with her uncle James Leonard and his wife, Cookie. After several weeks of thinking and mulling over all the possibilities, Patricia made a decision. Donald had also made his own decision. He moved out of the apartment they all shared into one room in a boarding house. It appears there was no hope that the marriage could be saved.

One day Terri went with her mother to an office. While her mother was talking to an attorney, Terri stayed with the secretary who showed the little girl how she could type her name using the manual typewriter. Terri worked very hard to type. When her mother came out of the office, Patricia had tears in her eyes but she didn't explain why. She did smile at Terri's typing attempts and said she was very proud of her efforts.

A few months later, Patricia made arrangements to move to Niles, Michigan. She found a job that paid enough for her to rent a remodeled Quonset hut to live in. She also made plans for her daughters to stay with Uncle James Leonard and Aunt Cookie on a farm where they lived and worked. The girls didn't understand why they had to live there without Mommy. But they were excited when they were told there were chickens and a cat and dog. A few months earlier, Terri had been treated for Rheumatic fever and was still following the doctor's orders for rest and good food. Living out in the country seemed to be a good solution to some of the problems.

Patricia worked and saved her money. She was hoping to go to business school, get a better paying job, and get her girls back with her. She had no idea how long it would take but she was determined. In spite of Patricia's knowledge of Uncle James Leonard's behavior with her which included some sexual abuse, she really didn't think any harm would come to her own little girls. He had always told her that she was special to him and that **_he loved only her in that special way._** And Patricia believed what he said – just as she had when she was a child.

By now Bill Drain had relocated to California. His youngest daughter, Kathleen, refused to live with him and his new wife. She was welcomed into Aunt Lucille's home and began a new way of living. Patricia's other sister, Bettie, had married and Cousin Norma was dating a doctor. All their lives seemed to be settling down again to a more normal routine.

In the early part of 1953, the divorce was final. Patricia had already moved out. Donald was trying to make amends with Leonette. She couldn't understand why he broke his family apart. One evening, he went back to the same restaurant in Logans Square in Chicago that he used to frequent. He had invited a woman out for a dinner date. The hostess he had often talked with, (who had a daughter a couple of years older than his daughter, Terri,) still worked there. She waited on him and was introduced to his date. She slipped her phone number to him by putting a slip of paper in his menu. They talked on the telephone several times after that evening. He asked her out for coffee and they talked. He assured her that he was divorced, because she told him she would not be involved with a married man. Her first husband had cheated on her and it had broken up the marriage. They dated for a few months and they got married in August, 1953. Donald now had a new wife and a new daughter. But he couldn't forget he was also the father to the three little girls who were living in another state.

In the meantime, Donald's sister, Virginia and her husband Emerson still did not have any children. They were living in Minonk, IL. Emerson was managing the grocery store across the street from their pretty house. Virginia had always been very fond of Terri and had purchased adorable little dresses for her when Terri was still a toddler. They asked Patricia if Terri could spend a couple of weeks with them in the summer. Terri could also see her Aunt Catherine, Uncle Russell and spent time with her cousins. After the visit, they asked if Terri could live with them permanently in Minonk, IL. Patricia did not want to split her children up and refused to separate her three girls. She didn't tell anyone it was because she had been separated from her own brothers and her birth father. She just couldn't bear the idea that the same thing could happen to her own little girls. She also didn't want anyone to know about her twin and her older brother and her father because she believed there was something wrong with her because she had been rejected by her own family members.

During the next two summers, Terri was allowed to visit her Aunt Virginia and Uncle Emerson and spend time with Aunt Catherine, Uncle Russell, and all her cousins. Aunt Virginia and Uncle Emerson finally had some babies of their own. Terri liked to help take care of the little ones.

During one visit, her father, Donald, came to Minonk to attend his high school reunion. He and his new wife, Dorothy, took Terri to the reunion picnic. She was beginning to forget about him because he was not part of her daily life. It took a few hours to feel any connection. It was difficult to feel close to him even though she resembled him and knew he was her father. She couldn't help but be a bit angry with him. He had left her and she felt rejected by him because of that. Even though his new wife, Dorothy, was very kind to Terri, she just felt uncomfortable with this woman who was married to her father. Terri knew plenty of other little girls whose fathers lived with them and didn't understand why she couldn't have a live-in father too.

The last summer Terri visited her Aunt Virginia began a period of darkness in her life. It started the day Uncle James Leonard came to pick her up from Aunt Virginia's house. He had come without any notice to take her home. She didn't understand why she had to leave before the planned visit was over. And then she didn't understand what he was doing to her on that ride home but she knew it was wrong. And worst of all, she knew she had to live with him until her mother could afford to take the girls back home to live with her. Terri was very confused.

The sexual abuse continued for what seemed like several years but was probably about three years in all. Terri didn't speak of it to anyone, including her mother and even her best girl friend. It remained a dark part of her life that she didn't like to discuss. It always brought up memories that she tried to bury within herself.

After a few months of saving, Patricia was able to move into the YWCA in South Bend, Indiana. South Bend was only a few hours away from the farm so she was still close to her little girls. She had a job and also attended a business school. A few months later, she was hired by General Motors Acceptance Corporation in a secretarial position. She didn't know how to drive and she certainly couldn't afford a car so she had to find a place that was on a bus line. Uncle James Leonard would pick her up on weekends a couple of times a month so she could visit with her girls. Sometimes she took a Greyhound bus back and forth to see them. It wasn't the best solution but it was a way to see the girls. Patricia was hopeful that the future would bring her girls back to her again.

    Uncle James Leonard usually took Terri along when he picked up her mother. The drive took a couple of hours. His excuse was that he couldn't go inside the YWCA to get Patricia so Terri had to get her. It was during those rides that some of the abuse took place. Terri finally got the courage to tell Uncle James Leonard that she was going to tell her mother. He smirked at her and smugly told her that her mother used to do the same things with him and that Patricia wouldn't care. Of course, being a child, Terri believed him. And so, she didn't tell anyone. But she did start becoming car sick and would often vomit in the car. It didn't stop the abuse.

    By this time Uncle James Leonard and Aunt Cookie had moved a few times themselves. They usually worked on a farm and had a house provided as part of the pay. They moved from Niles, Michigan to Rochester, Indiana, and then to Royal Center, Indiana while the girls lived with them.

    Terri and Ginny had the opportunity to attend a one room school for a school year. They liked the school bus and the school itself. They especially liked the hot lunch that was brought to the school every day by a school township bus. Their very favorite school hot lunch was turkey and gravy and mashed potatoes. They had a lot of friends at school and thrived on the farm lifestyle. They also liked having the cats and dogs for pets. They played outside most of the time and enjoyed the fresh air and home cooking.

Aunt Vernice was such a good cook that she had acquired the nickname "Cookie" early in her marriage. Terri told her one day that she knew why that was her name. When Aunt Vernice asked why, Terri said, "Well, because you are a good cooker!"

Uncle Jim and Aunt Cookie had never had children of their own. They had fostered a little boy named Timmy when he was about a year old. But his mother refused to let them adopt him, and took Timmy back to her home. In spite of very little experience with young children, Aunt Cookie was very good to the girls. Aunt Cookie encouraged them to play and sing and dress up. For Christmas, she made doll clothes for the few dolls the girls had, using an old treadle Singer sewing machine. She saved little scraps of feed bags and sewed little quilts for the dolls. Sometimes, the girls dressed the various kittens and puppies, who seemed to appear on a regular basis, in the doll clothes. But the girls always missed their mother, especially Terri and Ginny, who remembered her best.

Patricia continued to look for better employment. She worked for GMAC in South Bend for a short period. Then, she got a job as a proof reader for the *South Bend Tribune*. She would read the news articles and make corrections in the grammar, spelling, sentence construction, or any other visual mistake before the newspaper articles were printed.

She was also able to find an affordable apartment that was large enough for her and the three girls. It was upstairs in a converted attic of a huge older home. It was across the street from Memorial Hospital. It had a small kitchen and bathroom. There was a combination living room and dining area. The large bedroom held two single beds and a double bed. Even better, it was only a few blocks from a grocery store, a church, an elementary school, a laundromat, a doctor, a drugstore, and about six blocks from the library. She was ready to bring her children home to live with her.

South Bend, In. - 1955

The girls were all enrolled in school at James Madison Elementary in South Bend. Patricia had found a neighborhood woman who had two daughters and a son. Katie was willing to take care of the girls after school and keep Bonnie at her home half a day before Bonnie went to afternoon kindergarten. Katie provided a home-cooked lunch for the girls because there was no lunch program at school. Terri and Katie's oldest daughter, Vawnlea, became good friends. Kathy, her second daughter, and Ginny were about the same age. All the children were happy to play together on a daily basis. When school was not in session, the girls could still stay at Katie's house.

The girls enjoyed attending school at James Madison Elementary. It was only two blocks away. All the children in the neighborhood walked to and from school. Most of the neighborhood children played together. They played Kick the Can, Red Rover, Hide and Seek, Tag, Cowboys and Indians. The girls roller skated around the block. On Main Street where Terri, Ginny and Bonnie lived, the sidewalk pitched enough that they could just stand on the skates and glide down the sidewalk. If they were rolling too fast, they just steered into the grass. There was a hill with an alley behind their apartment building. In the winter, all the children got their sleds and went down the incline. The alley could get very icy, which was perfect for the sleds. Sometimes the children couldn't stop the sleds and would slide into the street. It ran into the back of the YWCA building where Patricia had lived a few years earlier. It was also close to James Madison Elementary School. As far as Terri can recall, no one ever got hit by a car even though the street was busy and the alley was hidden! The only serious problem the children suffered there was when Ginny fell off a swing at school and broke her left arm. She had to spend the night in Memorial Hospital. Even though it was across the street, Terri and Bonnie were worried about her. The sisters had never been apart so it was strange to them that Ginny wasn't there. She did come home the next day and her cast was admired by the entire neighborhood.

Life went on, books were read, music was listened to, and games were played in the apartment. One night the entire family came home after dark and when they opened the door and started up the steps to the attic living room, a bat flew over their heads. There was lots of screaming. Eventually, another tenant hit the bat with a broom and took it outside.

By now Patricia felt she was doing a good job as a mother and felt very responsible for her children. They still walked everywhere. She had a big wagon that was used to transport laundry, groceries, and tired children to and from the library downtown. She had a few friends, reliable people to care for her girls when she was working and even had a date or two.

After dating one man for several months, she thought it might be leading to a marriage. Jack Faust had taken her and her girls on a few day trips to visit her ex-sisters-in-law, Virginia and Catherine, her ex-mother-in-law, Leonette, and her Uncle James Leonard and Aunt Cookie. He seemed to want to take care of her and her girls as his own.

One Sunday, he told her he had a surprise. He picked up the entire family and drove them to Niles, Michigan where he proudly showed them a little house that he was buying. He topped off the special trip with milkshakes for everyone. He planned to propose to Patricia that evening. Perhaps it was an omen...but....Bonnie being a little girl, accidentally spilled and then dropped her shake all over the back seat of his car. Jack lost his temper, yelled at Bonnie and of course, Bonnie cried. Terri and Ginny were shocked into silence. They had never been screamed at before. Patricia did not say a word except to say **"Please take us home**." She broke off the relationship with Jack. She was sure she would never find a man who would be willing to take on her family and she wasn't even sure if she wanted to take another chance.

The girls continued to enjoy school and their neighborhood friends. Patricia had a few more dates. About 1956, Patricia was able to move her little family to the basement apartment of the same rental house which had two bedrooms and a larger kitchen with an eat-in area. The small bathroom only had a shower, sink, and toilet. The apartment took up about one third of the basement area. They also were given a portion of the basement storage area which was right outside their kitchen door. There wasn't a lot of light because there was only a small basement window in each bedroom and another small window in the kitchen. The neighborhood was still a nice family area. The children could play outside even in the evening and no one ever locked their doors in those days anyway.

Peggy was a neighborhood high school senior who was hired by Patricia to come in the morning and make sure the girls were up for school. Patricia had to take a bus to get to work by 7:00 A.M. Peggy would make breakfast for the girls and then get the older girls on their way to school and drop Bonnie at Katie's house. Occasionally, Peggy would also baby-sit in the evening if Patricia had a dinner date. Peggy would make dinner, play with the girls and once they were asleep, Peggy would leave.

Patricia was a lovely and attractive woman. She enjoyed the company of gentlemen callers. It was wonderful to see a movie, discuss books and music, and go dancing…all the things unrelated to being a single mother of three daughters. She looked forward to having dinner out especially because she didn't have to pay. It gave her more money out of her paycheck to take care of her children. One evening, Patricia arrived home about 11:00 P.M. She opened the door and smelled gas! Of course, she was frantic and woke up her girls to get them outside into the fresh air. The two bedroom windows were opened and the apartment was aired out. For several weeks after that incident, Patricia was afraid to go out in the evening, leaving her girls home. It took time for her to feel the girls were safe without her.

Terri wanted to learn to iron and Patricia allowed her to practice on handkerchiefs and pillowcases. Once she was good at that, Patricia let her iron the girls' blouses and dresses. In those days, Terri had to sprinkle the clothes the night before. She used an old Orange Nehi glass bottle and a sprinkler top and dampened all the clothes. She put them in a pillow case to keep them damp. Then the next evening, Terri would iron while Patricia made supper. The laundry was usually done on a Saturday afternoon and Sunday was the day to dampen the clothes, making Monday the ironing day. It was a special time that Terri enjoyed sharing with her mother.

Patricia had never learned to cook. Her mother had not taken the time to teach her how to do housework or to make a meal from scratch. When she lived with Leonette, she didn't have to cook either. Patricia learned to make a few simple recipes. She tried to include a vegetable with dinner and to always have a dessert, even if it was Jell-O. However, she never stirred the Jell-O up enough so the bottom was always rubbery. As a result, Jell-O with a rubbery base is a favorite in the family because it brings back a great memory. All her daughters remembered the famous cherry flavored rubbery Jell-O.

When there was a little extra money, Patricia would buy pudding to cook. Patricia always scorched the milk for vanilla pudding. That flavor is one that is recalled by some family members – but not with pleasure.

One evening, Patricia must have been very tired and Terri talked back when she was asked to help dry the dishes. Patricia said, "Damm it, just do it!" and slapped Terri across the face. Both of them burst into tears and immediately apologized to each other. It was the first and last time, Terri talked back to her mother and Patricia never EVER raised a hand to Terri again. To say that this little family of four females was non-aggressive and innocent in the ways of the world speaks volumes.

Patricia did not have much money to spare. She provided love and entertainment with records, music, books from the library, and games. Often the whole family would dance around to music on the record player.

Patricia loved Edith Piaf, the famous French singer. The girls could never understand the French songs which sounded very depressing. Terri always thought one was called "MAY I KILL PA." Another favorite record the girls liked to dance to was SLAUGHTER ON 10TH AVENUE which was a ballet by Richard Rodgers.

The girls often played with a small bag of colored blocks, their old dolls, and some board games. It didn't take a lot to keep them entertained. One of Terri's favorite things was an old catalog. She would cut out clothes and furniture for hours and make believe she was a fashion designer. She made paper dolls out of the illustrations and cut out an enormous number of outfits for them. She also was the designated paper doll clothes cutter for her sisters.

The girls had a few well-worn books that were read over and over. (Terri treasures a *Better Homes and Gardens Second Storybook* that Leonette gave her on December 16, 1952 which is sitting in her bookcase to this day). But the best time was going to the library downtown and bringing home books. The anticipation was nearly as good as the final selection.

Halloween was a special holiday because it was Beggars Night on October 30th and then regular Halloween on the next night. The neighborhood was usually generous to all the children. The upstairs tenants loved to have the girls show off their costumes which were homemade each year. The girls would spend weeks planning the costume, saving their allowance to buy crepe paper, and borrowing their mother's makeup and skirts to create their illusions. But usually Halloween would be so cold and rainy that the magnificent outfit had to be covered up by an old winter coat. Nevertheless, the candy was delicious!

One year, Christmas came when money was extremely tight. Donald normally was very faithful about sending child support. He had written to let Patricia know that he had not been working and had no money to spare. With everything she had to pay monthly, Patricia had only a little left for gifts for her girls. She talked to Terri about the problem and told her about a plan. Patricia took the Madame Alexander dolls that each girl had been given so many years before, to a doll "hospital" to be cleaned and re-wigged. "Nina the Ballerina" had dark curly brunette hair, "Fifi the French Girl" had a dark brunette ponytail, and "Susie the American Girl" had dark brunette curls just like the little girls who owned the dolls. The dolls had been well-loved and were in poor shape. Patricia waited until Christmas Eve and bought a small rejected fir tree for a few pennies. **It could have been the original Charlie Brown tree!** The girls understood that there wasn't any extra money.

That same year, Terri had saved up her allowance and had just over $1.00. She went to the neighborhood pharmacy to pick out the tiniest bottle of Evening in Paris perfume. The bottle probably held less than a 1/4 ounce of fragrance. The bottle was so beautiful. It was a cobalt blue glass container and it had a little dark purple tassel. She told the pharmacy owner she wanted to buy it for her mother for Christmas and carefully counted out all the pennies and nickels in her pocket. Years later, she remembered that the kind drugstore owner told her she had **just enough money** to make her purchase. Terri is sure that the perfume cost much more than the few pennies she had managed to save.

The girls saved used Christmas cards each year to cut out to decorate the white tissue paper that was the annual gift wrap. With a bit of crinkle ribbon, the packages looked very nice.

Patricia always saved up money for an Easter outfit for each girl to wear to church. The First Methodist Church was only a few blocks from home. The girls usually got an outfit or two at the beginning of the school year and a pair of new shoes. Often, the clothes were hand-me-downs from Terri to Ginny. Bonnie was a little chubbier than the other two and so, she had to get special clothing from the children's department at Lane Bryant. Patricia would wait for a sale in the hopes of finding something that would be affordable for Bonnie to wear. Bonnie also needed some special shoes and although they were expensive, they did last a long time.

One Easter, Terri had a grey suit jacket with a matching pleated skirt and a pink checked blouse and Ginny and Bonnie had matching navy blue suit jackets with pleated skirts and blue checked blouses. They all looked so nice on Easter Sunday. And what was even better was the next year, Ginny could wear the grey outfit.

_1957_

Terri was in 7th grade. She was asked to help the afternoon kindergarten teacher with the children during her study hall. She enjoyed being with the children. At the end of the year, the principal gave her a little pin with the initials of JMES (James Madison Elementary School) as a thank you for helping. That same year, Terri helped with a newspaper the 7th grade created and printed and distributed. She wrote a couple of articles and also won the contest to name the paper. She submitted the name of **_Junior Hi-lights_**. She helped to put the paper together for distribution. The group of students spent a few afternoons after school putting the paper together. Was she following in the writing footsteps of her female ancestors?

About that same time, Patricia started dating a man who also worked for the _South Bend Tribune_. He was the Business and Labor Editor. He was several years older than Patricia and was divorced. He had a grown daughter and son. He had been living alone for many years. The couple got along quite well and had similar interests. He was introduced to the three girls and seemed to greatly enjoy the family of females. He took them to see the

Tulip Festival in Holland, Michigan one spring. He took them to Chicago to see the Museum of Science and Industry and the Field Museum. He paid for the girls to go to the movies occasionally on a Saturday afternoon. He also attended the same church the little family went to every Sunday morning. He lived in a downtown hotel. He had a car. He enjoyed the theater and music and art and traveling.

He invited Patricia to go on a couple of weekend trips. The girls stayed with Uncle Jim and Aunt Cookie while their mother was out of town. Naturally, the girls didn't like the fact that this man was intruding in their lives and taking their mother's attention away. They were used to being a family of females.

Terri especially did not like staying on the farm because Uncle Jim continued to abuse her. She tried to stay away from him. There were times when she had no choice but to go in the car with him. Every Sunday, he drove to town to get the newspaper and that was when Terri had to go along. She even thought if she invited her best friend, Vawnlea, to go to the farm that Uncle Jim would leave her alone but it didn't work out that way.

Terri was sure that Aunt Cookie knew what was going on because she started blaming Terri when the girls misbehaved even if Terri wasn't involved with the other two little girls' disagreements. Terri again threatened to tell her mother. Uncle Jim just laughed and said he used to do the same things to Patricia so he knew she wouldn't care. Of course, Terri believed him and didn't tell her mother until many, many years later when she was grown. He also told Terri if she didn't cooperate with him that he would turn to her sisters.

There were a few times when Terri saw him with her sisters and he looked her right in the eyes as if to say "See, I can do it to them easily too!" Terri always felt responsible for her younger sisters and, of course, she decided that her sisters should not ever be in the situation she was in. It wasn't until Terri was about 48 years old that she realized how much she had believed what he said so many years before. She never thought that she could tell her mother at the time it was happening or even change the outcome. Years later, her sisters told her that they knew what he was doing to her but didn't know what to do to stop it.

***
Friday, July 31, 1955

Dearest Pat:
I dream of you, I cherish you...
Each second of each hour...
To me you are the petal and...
The fragrance of each flower...
You are the silver stars that are...
The sentinels of the night...
You are the dawn when fear is gone...
You are my sunshine bright...
You are the hopes that fill my heart...
You are the one and only one...
I ever want to treasure...
To you I give my loving heart...
My life forever more...
With all the joys I own today...
And all that are in store...
I only want your happiness...
Forever and forever...
I only want to be with you...
And never leave you never.

Again Metcalfe took the words right out of my mouth.

Love Ray
***

Although Raymond was not very thrifty with money, he did enjoy traveling. In the early years of their relationship, there were times he and

Patricia took a weekend trip on their own. The girls were taken to Uncle Jim and Aunt Cookie's to stay. The girls didn't like going there so often but they realized that sometimes it was just too expensive for the whole group to travel together at the same time. Terri had her own reasons for not wanting to go to the farm but she vowed she would go if only to watch over her younger sisters. After all, she had constantly been told that because she was the oldest, it was her responsibility to be sure her sisters were safe and she was supposed to keep them out of trouble.

The joy of having lots of dogs and cats to play with on the farm was still a special experience. They each "adopted" an outside kitten of their own and named them Tommy, Fluffo, and Kitty. Those poor little kittens were subjected to being dressed in doll clothes. The animals would play with the girls for hours without running away. There were also a couple of dogs to play with, along with a litter of puppies from time to time.

The girls learned to pick wild raspberries and had them on breakfast cereal and on homemade ice cream at night. They also helped pick strawberries from the few little plants Aunt Cookie put out. They learned to pull weeds in the garden. They helped hang the laundry on the lines outside and still had plenty of time to play in the attic which had no furniture. They kept their dolls and comic books, paper dolls, and old catalogs to cut up and create homes for their doll families in the attic too. They slept in a downstairs unheated bedroom – all three in the same bed. It was cozy and warm with all three of them in the same bed. Terri and Ginny slept side by side and Bonnie slept horizontally across the bottom of the bed. Bonnie was like their own private foot warmer.

On Saturday night, it was time to go to town to the grocery store and to the local 5 & 10 to buy new paper dolls, comic books, or coloring books, and of course, the Trixie Belden books. 25 to 50 cents went a very long way in those days. The girls were allowed to shop for their treasures while Uncle James Leonard and Aunt Cookie went to the grocery store.

One winter evening, the girls were waiting in the car while Uncle James Leonard and Aunt Cookie were grocery shopping. Terri was in the back seat with her two sisters when she realized the car was moving backward. She jumped into the front seat and put her foot on the brake. As the car finally slowed and then stopped, a man opened the driver's door and asked if the girls were alright. Another customer went into the store to find Uncle James Leonard. The whole experience frightened Terri so much that she didn't learn to drive until she was 30 years old. She had nightmares about being in the back seat of a moving car and not being able to stop the car for many years after that incident. In every dream, there was someone else in the car that she had to protect.

The Gregg Years

Finally, Ray proposed and Patricia accepted. Ray and Patricia were married on July 6, 1958. He took her on a honeymoon trip to California so she could see her dear Aunt Lucille and her sister, Bettie. They moved to a two-story duplex on Grandview Ave. across the street from Colfax Elementary School. Terri was going to be in 8th grade and would go to Central High School. It had grades 8th through 12th. Ginny and Bonnie would attend Colfax School right across the alley from their new home.

Terri had a bedroom of her own and the other two girls shared a room. It seems as if life was going to be very good for the new family of five. Maybe the hard times were finally over. A few months later, Uncle James Leonard and Aunt Cookie moved far enough away that visiting wasn't an option as often. And as the girls got older, they were allowed to stay home by themselves when Patricia and Raymond were out for the evening.

Raymond and Patricia continued their jobs with the newspaper. They both worked on Saturday and had Sunday and Monday off. This was a good arrangement because Terri could be responsible for the other two girls on Saturday. Patricia usually left a small list of chores for the girls to do. This kept them busy for a short while, they helped around the house and still had time to read and enjoy their Saturday.

One rainy overcast Saturday morning, Terri came out of her bedroom and saw Bonnie packing her little doll suitcase. At first Terri thought Bonnie was playing with her dolls. Then she noticed that 8 year old Bonnie had put in a pair of shorts, an undershirt, some comic books, and a peanut butter & jelly sandwich wrapped awkwardly in waxed paper. Terri asked

Bonnie what she was doing. She noticed Bonnie had some pennies and a nickel on her bed.

"I'm going to run away." Bonnie said very importantly and proudly. "I don't want to live here anymore."

Terri was surprised and asked "But why?"

Bonnie said "I just don't want to be here anymore. I'll go somewhere else to live."

"Bonnie, where will you go? It's rainy and cold outside." Terri asked.

By this time, Ginny had come into the bedroom she shared with Bonnie. Ginny also asked "Why do you want to run away? Are you mad at someone?"

"No, but I don't like it here." Bonnie said again.

Terri told Bonnie "You know, Mom will be so worried and sad. She will probably cry a lot because you are not here. Can't you stay and talk about it to us?"

"Nooooo! I want to leave right now!" Bonnie insisted.

Terri was really afraid that Bonnie would walk out the door and what in the world would Terri tell their mother if Bonnie was gone.

Finally, Terri said to Bonnie. "Please don't leave yet. Let's have lunch and play together for awhile.

Then when Mom comes home, you can tell her why you want to leave."

Bonnie thought for a moment and agreed. Thankfully that problem was over, at least for that year. It became a typical response in Bonnie. She sometimes reacted to difficulties by running away from her problems in life. It took her a very long time to learn to face the problems and stay in one place.

One afternoon, Terri, Ginny, and Bonnie were walking downtown to the library. As they passed the neighborhood A&P grocery store, they read the sign in the window.

Suddenly, Terri said "Oh my goodness, Mom won a turkey!"

They ran all the way home and told Patricia the great news. Patricia picked up the free turkey which they had for Thanksgiving. This turned out to be a real blessing because money was sometimes tight for the family. In spite of having two paychecks, after paying rent, food, utilities, and buying other necessities, there was not often much left over.

The girls walked to the library nearly every Saturday. The library was in an old building. To the girls, it resembled a small castle with turrets. It was very fairy tale like in structure. The Children's Department was upstairs and had huge tall windows with window seats between the book stacks. There were little cubbyholes where you could sit with your books and just read before the long walk back home. It was a proud day when you could write your name and get your very own library card!!! Terri loved the whole procedure of checking out the books. The librarians had a special pencil. The procedure was so organized and efficient with not a moment wasted. The date stamper was attached to the back of the pencil and the librarian could quickly stamp the book card, remove it from the back of the book, and put the due date card in the book. Terri considered the thought of becoming a librarian when she grew up. In later years, if she would have had the money for college; she would have studied to get a degree in Library Science.

    Another Saturday, there was a knock at the door. It was a delivery man from Sears and Roebuck. He had a big package that he left on the porch because the girls told him they were not allowed to let anyone in when their parents were gone. It was a small desk and chair for Terri's 13th birthday. She used the desk and chair until the day she got married. It was her work desk and her makeup table. It held a lot of treasures during the years. She left it in her old room for her sisters to use once she had moved out.

1959

The family was settling into a routine but they wanted a home of their own. Raymond and Patricia found a three bedroom home in a nice neighborhood. They purchased the house and moved in during the summer of 1959.

Terri had her own room. She had the trundle bed that she and Patricia had shared so long ago. (A trundle is a bunk bed with the lower bed sliding under the top bed.) She had her little desk and chair, a bookcase, and a tiny closet. It was cozy but small. As a teenager, she especially enjoyed having her own space and privacy. Ginny and Bonnie shared a bedroom with their original regular bunk beds. They also had a dresser by now and a large open closet for their clothes and precious possessions.

The kitchen had an eat-in area which was very snug for 5 people. The kitchen cupboards were white enameled metal. There was no counter space. There was only one white enameled metal base cabinet unit which held the kitchen sink.

During that time period, Ray and Patricia took out a home improvement loan and expanded the house. There was a fair sized front and back yard. They had the kitchen window taken out to make room for a large doorway. From that point, they had a large room built onto the back of the house which was used as a family room and dining area. They put in a large closet on one side of the passageway and a washer and dryer on the other side. It always amused Terri that the dryer would play **HOW DRY I AM** when the laundry was dry. The new room had a linoleum floor, built in bookcases on one side, two rows of windows for lots of sunlight, and was the main place where the family gathered every day for meals and to watch television.

Throughout the years, Raymond took the family to the East to Maine, New York, Virginia Beach, Virginia, and as far West as California. They went to Yellowstone National Park, the Grand Canyon, San Francisco, and other well known vacations spots including Canada.

The plan was always that the family would camp. Each trip, the tent, sleeping bags, food, and other necessities were packed into the car. But usually after a night or two in the tent, Raymond's back would bother him and they would stay in a motel. In those days, finding a motel with a pool was the biggest concern. The girls loved to swim in the pool to cool off. There was no air conditioning in the car so the hot weather really wore everyone out. They did eat picnic lunches and breakfasts with the food they brought along. They once stayed in a cabin for a week in Yellowstone National Park and cooked outside every day. They rode the cable cars in San Francisco to the end of the line and jumped off as the cable car turned and rode it back up to the other end. They drove down the winding streets in San Francisco. They went to Chinatown and ate in a real Chinese restaurant. They also ate wonderful seafood on both the West and East Coasts.

That fall, Terri started 10th grade at John Adams High School. She had to take a bus to and from school. She occasionally walked home but it was a long walk after being in school all day. The other two sisters went to Thomas Edison Elementary school, which was just a few blocks away.

Terri had a good high school experience. She had started out at Central High School which was near the downtown area of her home town. She especially loved the magnolia blossoms that appeared every spring. It was so beautiful to see the white and pink flowers appear. When they fell off the trees, there was a gorgeous carpet of blossoms for a few more days. She did well in school, not Honor Society good - but in the upper one third of the class.

In her sophomore year, she transferred to John Adams High School because the family had purchased their home in that school district. On her first day at John Adams High School, she went into her home room and met her future husband! **Of course; she didn't know it at that time!** She was greeted by a girl named Lynda who showed her around and introduced Terri to Lynda's good friend since elementary school.

His name was Dean. He had dark brown eyes and dark curly hair. He was very friendly. It wasn't too long before Terri had a crush on him, but of course, he had no idea. She used to write his name in code on her English book (which was a fad at that time). She and Lynda became good friends. They were Spanish class partners and Office Practice partners and English classmates. Lynda was always trying to get Dean to talk to Terri because she was sure they would make a perfect couple!

Terri did wonder if she would reach the age of **"sweet 16 and never been kissed"** when she went into her junior year. She was asked out on a few dates by Bob. He took her to the movies a couple of times and introduced her to his sister. And even more importantly, he gave her a kiss before she was 16. In fact, he kissed her several times. Unfortunately, Bob was dating other girls at the same time. Terri's heart was broken when her best friend, Vawnlea, told her that Bob was dating another girl and that it appeared to be "serious" between them.

Terri was asked out on a few dates by a young man who was in the Navy. He was on leave visiting his cousin, Dwayne. Dwayne, was dating a friend of Terri's. They went to a party and a movie together. John was home only for a short time. He was much too old and experienced for Terri. So she wasn't too upset when his leave was over. She really didn't want to be pressured into any type of relationship or situation that she wasn't comfortable with.

In her senior year, she had a crush on another boy but he never asked her out although they flirted every day in Government class. Another friend tried to get him to ask Terri to the Winter Wonderland Dance but he never did. Terri had not had a date for several months and was surprised to learn from some of her friends that many of the boys thought she was still dating Bob. That had been over for a year. In fact, Bob had a steady girlfriend by that time. It was the same girl that Vawnlea told Terri about earlier the previous year. In fact, he married that girl when she became pregnant several months later.

1961

     That spring, Patricia became quite ill. She had strep throat and was sick in bed for several days. She just couldn't seem to get over the exhausted feelings and she felt nauseous too. When it continued, she went to the doctor. What he told her was a real shock!

     That night Raymond and Patricia told the girls that there was going to be a baby in December. All the girls were excited about having a baby in the family. It had been a very long time since the last one. They teased Bonnie about not being the baby sister any more. They all discussed the best name for the new baby that would be coming in a few months. The girls teased their mother by suggesting the middle name should be her maiden name of Hill. Choices like Tower Hill or Sandy Hill were suggested.

As the time approached for the birth, the girls' bedrooms were switched. Terri and Ginny would share a bedroom and a new set of beds. The beds looked like couches and there was a table to fit in the corner so the beds made up an "L" shape. It made the room look more grownup. Bonnie would move into the little middle bedroom with the trundle beds because a crib would fit in there too.

Finally the big day came on December 5th, 1961 and another daughter joined the family. Her name was Mary Rachel. She was named after Raymond's mother and of course, Rachel was a substitute for Raymond. In the months following her birth, her name was often shortened to Mary Rae which Raymond loved.

Raymond had come home from the hospital that morning with a few Polaroid pictures. He told the girls they could stay home from school but all three of them wanted to go to tell their friends at school about the new baby.

Eventually, Patricia went back to work part-time on Saturdays at the newspaper and once again, the girls did household chores and took care of Mary on the days that Patricia worked. One day, Terri had just changed Mary's diaper. Mary was on the top part of the trundle bed. Mary suddenly turned over and fell to the floor about four feet below. The girls were scared. They checked her over and didn't see any bruises but they were worried. They checked with the next door neighbor who had six children. She told them to keep her awake the rest of the day but if she started to fall asleep to call Patricia at work. She was fine and Terri told her mother when Patricia got home that afternoon.

Needless to say, Raymond was very proud to have a baby girl at his age. He was 55 years old and Patricia was nearly 39. He carried Mary Rae all over when they were in public. Sometimes, people asked if he was the grandfather, which upset him. The girls thought it was funny that either the sisters or Patricia always took care of Mary but as soon as they were at a restaurant or at church, or in public; Raymond was holding her.

In March of 1962, Terri was in the last semester of her senior year in high school. She was in Sociology Class with Dean. Every Friday, a student would be called upon to discuss Current Events. Her teacher had asked her privately if she would be willing to talk about something a bit unusual that most students don't experience. She was willing and was called upon that Friday.

It did seem weird to stand up in front of everyone in the class and talk about the event. It is something that most people don't go through especially at the age of 17. But Terri thought it would be interesting to the rest of her classmates. And even better, it might get her a good grade in class that day!

So, she told everyone how her stepfather, Ray, had asked the St. Joseph Probate Court to change the last name of Terri, Ginny and Bonnie to his last name so all four girls, including the new baby, Mary Rachel, would have the same last name. Terri described what the court room was like. She explained that the judge asked her if she was willing to change her name since she was older than 16 years and had "rights." On March 8, 1962, her name changed legally and would be Terri Jeanne Gregg until she married.

She was willing to change her name but inside she did feel some guilt. She loved her real father and felt that giving up his name was like giving him up. She did understand the reason for the name change. She had to admit that the new last name was much easier to spell and pronounce….but still...

Terri knew her mother had asked her birth father for permission and she also knew it meant Donald didn't have to pay child support anymore. But she still felt hurt, just a little, that her birth father was willing to give up his legal rights to his daughters. She wondered if she would ever have a relationship with him in her later life.

A couple of weeks later, Dean, who was in the same Sociology class, went out the door after class at the same time as Terri. He stopped her and asked if she would go to the Senior Prom with him! Terri's response was "Are you kidding? Yes!"

Dean walked her to her next class and told her he would discuss the details with her later. Terri floated through the rest of the day at school and could hardly wait to tell her mother when she got home. Both of them were very excited about this big event coming in a few weeks. Not only was this the first dance Terri would go to but it was the **SENIOR PROM,** one of the biggest events of the year.

At school, there was lots of discussion and plans for the prom and who and how and what and where they would go for that special time. Dean and Terri went bowling on an afternoon date and to a movie on their first evening date. By the time the Senior Prom came along in May, they were enjoying each other's company very much.

Terri found a very feminine pale yellow chiffon dress with little chiffon ruffled sleeves and a full knee-length skirt. She got shoes dyed to match and felt very pretty when she carefully dressed for the prom. Dean brought her a beautiful yellow orchid with red accents on it. Dean wore a tux with a white jacket and a red plaid cummerbund and handkerchief.

Dean and Terri - Senior Prom

    They went to the prom with another couple and had a great time. The after-party was at the First Methodist Church and then the next day most of the couples went to Tower Hill which is a beach in Michigan. The whole weekend flew by in seconds.

    It wasn't long after the prom that Dean and Terri started going steady. Terri wore Dean's class ring and wound long lengths of yellow angora yarn around it to keep it on her finger. Dean wore Terri's ring on a chain around his neck. They were happy to be a couple. Ray and Patricia liked Dean very much and approved of the relationship. That June Terri and Dean graduated from high school.

If you look closely, you can see the angora wrapped ring on Terri's hand.

After graduation, Terri decided she would attend a business school in the area. She attended The South Bend College of Commerce every weekday from 8:00 A.M. and got home about 3:00 P.M. She would do her homework which was to listen to radio broadcasts for about an hour and take down the conversation using Speedwriting which was a version of Shorthand. Then she would usually feed and play with Mary so Patricia could start dinner or have a break. Terri became very close to Mary and liked to play with her. In fact, all the girls took care of Mary and enjoyed teaching her new things. Mary Rae was very quick to learn and loved all the attention of her big sisters. Mary always could find someone who was willing to read her a story or play with her. Patricia got the Hooked on Phonics program and started teaching Mary the alphabet and words. She was soon able to read the newspaper or business signs. It was so fascinating for the girls to ask Mary to read when she was under three years of age. She could sound out almost every word and soon was as eager to learn as her sisters were to teach her.

A few weeks later, Terri started receiving letters from the boy she had a crush on in her Government class. He was in college in Moscow, Idaho and asked to see her when he came home for the holidays. She agreed but felt very confused. When he was due home, she told Dean she wanted to break up with him and think about their relationship. She just didn't feel right seeing that college boy and still going steady with Dean. He did come home and they went out for the evening. He told her he loved her and wanted to get married right away.

It should be noted DEAR READERS that the college boy and Terri had never been on a date!

He said he could take good care of her. He was going to be a National Park Forest Ranger. He told her that in about three years, they would live in the woods in a cabin in Idaho or Montana and have a wonderful life. When Terri hesitated and said she didn't want to leave her family and go so far away. He could not understand her hesitation. Terri asked him what would happen if she became pregnant and they were living in the woods. He said he would deliver the baby...no problem. That frightened her. Then he kissed her. And there was nothing in that kiss that made her feel a connection to him. He took her home, still talking about all the plans he had made. He really expected her to get married immediately and leave with him. He said she could get a job while he finished college to help support them. Then when he got his Forest Ranger job, they would be ready for a family. Terri avoided his phone calls for the next couple of days and then finally told him she didn't think it was going to work out. She said goodbye and wished him well. (In later years, he changed his plans. He had to leave college when the money ran out. He then enlisted in the Air Force and was stationed in Eastern Asia and in Vietnam. After his tour in the Air Force, he went back to Indiana, and completed college. He got his teaching certificate. He became a science teacher in his home town. He never became a Forest Ranger at all. He got married and divorced and then married a second time).

After Terri had told him goodbye, she wondered what she was going to do about Dean. She knew she loved him and since she had pushed him away, she was worried that he wouldn't talk to her.

Unbeknownst to Terri, Dean had been talking to her step-father. They both worked for the *South Bend Tribune* at that time. Ray had assured Dean that Terri would see what was right for both of them. Ray told Dean not to give up on the relationship.

A few days later, Terri finally got her courage up and called Dean. Fortunately, he answered the phone. She asked if he could come over so they could talk. He agreed. They did talk very seriously. She apologized for the breakup and told him what had happened. They got back together. They were more committed to a long-term relationship and worked together to make it right. They had plenty of long conversations about what they wanted out of life and how they could achieve those dreams.

About that time, there was a gasoline commercial with an animated dinosaur named Dino. Little Mary soon decided that Dean was her "Dino Darling." She would squeeze her tiny body in-between Dean and Terri when they were sitting on the couch. If Terri was still too close, Mary would tell her "Dino Darling" she wanted to sit on his lap and then smile smugly at Terri. She loved to have Dean carry her around whenever possible as well. She was loved by all her family including her very own "Dino Darling."

After a few more months, Dean and Terri talked more about the future. They both had full-time jobs. Dean worked as a courier delivering tear sheets for the *South Bend Tribune* and Terri worked as a secretary for Woodworth Storage and Transfer which was affiliated with Allied Van Lines. They were committed to the relationship. Dean asked Terri to marry him. They decided to make it official and got engaged.

    Terri and her father, Donald, had re-established a relationship after several years. Donald wrote to let her know that he had a business appointment in her town and invited her out to dinner. Terri accepted and they spend the evening catching up on all the news. Then, Donald drove Terri to a laundromat where Dean was doing his laundry. Donald was introduced to his future son-in-law.

1964

Dean and Terri were planning to get married in the fall of 1965. In Indiana, the legal age for men to be married was 21. Dean's birthday was August 31, 1944. He knew his parents would not give permission for a wedding before his 21st birthday so the couple would have to wait until autumn of 1965.

Just before New Year Eve in 1964, a friend of Terri's had eloped to Michigan and got married by a Justice of the Peace. Michigan was only about nine or ten miles from where Dean and Terri's families lived. They didn't think their parents would approve of eloping.

One day, Raymond asked Dean why they were waiting to get married when they could go to Michigan and get married at a Justice of the Peace. Terri talked to Dean on New Year's Eve 1964 about eloping. They discussed the pros and cons. They decided they would get married in April instead. Even though they would have liked to have a church wedding, they wanted to be married and out on their own even more.

But first Dean had to find a better job because the *Tribune* paid minimum wage and they couldn't support themselves even with both salaries. Also the *Tribune* would not allow the courier to be married for some reason. It was probably because the wage was so minimal. A few months later, Dean got a different job working nights and the wage per hour was much better.

Dean and Terri wanted to pay for the wedding and reception themselves. They decided to invite Terri's mother and sisters and Dean's two younger brothers to the ceremony. The Best Man was one of Dean's friends from work. The Matron of Honor was Lynda, who was Dean's long time friend and the one who introduced them in high school. Dean's parents did not attend. Raymond had to work.

Terri had been saving at least $25 a week ever since she started working and had $1000 saved up. They rented an apartment which had a community building they could use for the reception. They took Dean's stereo over to the building along with their favorite records to use as entertainment. Terri's parents paid for ice cream. Dean's mother made the wedding cake. Dean and Terri bought the decorations, the paper plates, some nuts and fancy mints, made the punch and put it all together.

They did get married on the morning of April 10, 1965 in Michigan. They spent the rest of the day getting the community building ready for the reception that evening. Friends of the couple, neighbors, family members, and a few relatives attended. Dean and Terri opened their gifts and thanked each person individually for coming to the reception and for the gifts as they went around the room. Dean and Terri left about 10:30 P.M. They spent their wedding night in Elkhart, Indiana. They got up very early Sunday morning to drive to Niagara Falls, Canada. It was lucky they left so early because that was the date of the famous Palm Sunday Tornado that went through later that morning and caused an amazing amount of damage.

On Monday morning, they woke up in their motel in Niagara Falls, and turned on the TV. All the national newscasts were about the big tornado in South Bend. They did not have a telephone in their room. They frantically got dressed and went out to find a payphone. Terri was so frightened when she called her mother. Patricia was frightened because she thought something had happened to the newlyweds. They sorted out the information and realized that everything was fine on both ends of the phone call. Dean and Terri continued their honeymoon in Canada until Wednesday and then went home to their very own apartment to settle in as a married couple.

Within the next year, they bought their first home. They were both still working, they had purchased a used convertible, and life was good. They got a white German shepherd for company. They thought they had it all, a home, a dog, and even a section of the white picket fence at the front of the house.

That white German shepherd turned out to be a blessing in disguise. One evening, Terri was home alone. There was a knock at the kitchen door. She opened it to see a man who claimed he was from the telephone company. He said there was a problem with the lines and he needed to come inside. Terri was about to let him in when the dog, who had been standing by her side, started to growl. His fur rose up and he stood up as his ears went back. Terri kept trying to quiet him. The man asked if the dog would bite. Terri said no. As the man started to enter the kitchen, the dog started barking. The dog started for the man. The man quickly left. Terri then realized that the man had not been wearing a uniform. She checked the street at the front of the house. There was no truck. Terri was sure that the man could have hurt her and may even have been watching her for a few days when she walked home from the bus stop. Thank goodness the dog had the right instincts.

A few months after that, a co-worker of Dean's asked the couple an important question. Would they consider moving to the Florida Keys? The co-worker's in-laws had a motel on one of the islands and wanted their daughter and son-in-law to move closer to them in Florida. The in-laws said there were lots of job opportunities there and the weather was great.

Dean and Terri discussed it and decided they were in a position to try it out as they had no children and no debts, except for the mortgage on the house. They sold the house and most of the furniture to a couple who took over the mortgage payments. Dean and Terri made plans to go. They both gave up good jobs, their home, their furniture, and their families to try a new adventure.

The co-worker and his wife had just had a newborn baby. Dean and his friend drove their belongings in a small trailer to the Keys during the first week of April so the men could start looking for their jobs. The baby's doctor wanted to see the baby for its 6th week checkup before they left the area. Terri moved in with the new mother for a week. The other couple had family in Islamorada in the Keys and would be staying at the motel her family owned. Terri traveled with the woman and two of the woman's friends and helped care for the baby on the trip. They drove straight through to Florida and arrived in the middle of the night.

Dean told Terri once she had arrived that the other couple's parents were not willing to give them a room at the motel or to help them find jobs. They would be on their own.

Dean had just rented an apartment the day before. They quickly got Terri's luggage and left to be alone again. They had been apart for this anniversary and were anxious to talk and reconnect since this was the first time they had been apart since they got married. Obviously, a lot of false promises had been made because the in-laws wanted their daughter and new grandson back home. Even though the other couple wanted Dean and Terri to stay and were sure they could work things out, there wasn't time to waste. Money was tight.

Dean had been looking for a job and actually got an offer a day after Terri arrived. However, it was on Marathon which was another island, and they had to move to that key. They were able to get back most of their rent and security deposit thanks to the assistance of a realtor who was originally from Indiana. She also found them a rental duplex to live in and even bought used furniture for them (the duplex belonged to her son-in-law). Dean started a job as a meter reader for the Electric Co-Op. Terri found a job about a week later at the only bank on the key. They soon were settling into a new place with great weather.

After about two months, they became aware that they were not getting anywhere. They didn't enjoy fishing and drinking as most of the people did. They worked their jobs. They took their laundry to an outdoor laundromat. They bought groceries. They spent time with a few couples they had met and played cards on the weekends. They drove to Key West to an outdoor theater about every three weeks as a treat.

Terri's parents had planned on a trip to visit them in Florida later that summer. One night, Terri had a strange dream about Uncle James Leonard. Soon after, her mother wrote a letter telling her that he had passed away. Terri checked the date and was sure she dreamed about him the night he died. Was it a visit from him? Aunt Cookie was not doing well emotionally and they feared she would have to be put into a mental hospital.

★★★

TO JIM

May twenty second, nineteen sixty seven
God called my uncle Jim to heaven
God said: "Your work on earth is through,
I've got a bigger job for you in Heaven, Jim"
Jim wasn't a man to quote poetry
Or the latest trend in Art.
But he liked the feel of the earth in his hands
And to know that he'd done his part...
to make this world a better place.
His heart was as big as all outdoors
Whatever he had to give was yours...
If you needed it.
So, when God said
"Jim, I need a man who's not afraid of hard work
Can you come?"
Jim said "I can!
Now the world's a little lonelier without him
But I'm sure, the Lord is happy to have a man... Like Jim.

Written by Patricia Gregg

***

BACK HOME AGAIN IN INDIANA

In late June, Terri and Dean decided that this Florida move just wasn't working out. All the things the other couple had promised them such as a place to stay inexpensively, a job, etc. had not panned out. At first, the couple invited them over to swim in the motel pool every weekend. Then, those invitations started to fade away. In fact, they hardly ever saw the other couple. So, they decided that instead of spending any more money, they would wait until their next payday and go home. And that is what they did.

On the way, they stopped for gasoline in Northern Florida. Dean was offered a job running a Marathon gas station with a small repair area. The owner was an older man and wanted to plan for his retirement. He offered to teach Dean everything he knew and then he said Dean could buy him out in a few years. The young couple was afraid to take a chance. All they had was a few dollars to get them home.

A few weeks earlier, Dean had also been interviewed for a job as a prison guard at one of the road labor camps run by the State. It meant that they had to live on the grounds and the couple was not sure that was a good idea because Terri would be home alone during the day. Terri didn't drive at that time so she would not have any way to drive to and from a job.

In later years, Dean and Terri often discussed what might have happened to their lives if they had taken either opportunity instead of going back to Indiana.

Finally, they got back home and moved in with Dean's parents for a few days. Both of them found jobs right away and found an apartment very quickly. They borrowed some used furniture from Dean's parents. Money was tight but they were glad to be home again.

They moved once again months later when Terri was offered her old job back with the moving and storage company. Dean took another job working for a gas station owner to have some cash coming in. It was long hours and not much pay.

Raymond approached Dean one day and asked if he ever thought about becoming a policeman. Dean didn't think he had a chance but he applied. To his great surprise, he was hired. He worked very hard while attending the police school and was proud to be sworn in and given his uniform and badge and gun in the autumn of 1967.

Dean's new job as a police officer meant there was more stability in Dean and Terri's life. They had medical insurance now and expected their jobs to last as long as they wanted to work. They started discussing having a family. Terri stopped taking her birth control pills and was pregnant within a few weeks. They were thrilled. The baby was due about the end of August, 1968, very close to Dean's birthday on August 31st. The baby would be the first grandchild in Terri's family.

A few months later, in 1968, Terri's sister Virginia (known as Ginny) graduated from college. Ginny was engaged to a man who was a high school history teacher. He had decided to go to medical school to become a doctor. The couple planned to get married in a couple of years. Ginny would work as a primary school teacher while he was in school. Then when he became an intern, she would move with him to the city where he was working.

Bonnie was a senior in high school but wanted to get away from home. She became involved in the McCarthy Presidential Campaign in South Bend and decided to quit high school and travel with the campaign around the country. Needless to say,

Raymond and Patricia were not very happy about that decision. Bonnie only had about three weeks of high school left but since she was 18 years of age, there was nothing Raymond and Patricia could do legally to stop her

During that summer, Bonnie was away from home, still traveling around the country for the McCarthy campaign. Ginny was teaching and planning her wedding and Mary was in elementary school. Patricia worked for the newspaper proof room on occasional weekdays and Saturdays and to fill in for vacations.

Dean and Terri enjoyed the pregnancy. Terri had a little bit of sickness but it was usually in the evening, not the morning. She continued to work and looked forward to wearing maternity clothes. She didn't tell her employers that she was pregnant until June because she wasn't sure they would let her keep her job. June was when she had to start wearing maternity clothes because she couldn't hide behind over blouses or full skirts any longer. She was the rate clerk and prepared the charges for local and long distance moves for Allied Van Lines. She had to weigh the semi trucks, go out into the storage area, handle phone calls, give estimates over the phone, and so on.

It was a busy and active job.

Terri's due date was the end of August, right around Dean's birthday. She planned to work as long as possible. In July, she was feeling the pregnancy and was tired enough to want to stay home and get prepared for the baby. They had a used crib, used stroller, and she even wore some of her mother's old maternity clothes. She also purchased a few items of her own. She bought cloth diapers because at that time, disposable diapers were just coming out and they were too expensive. She also bought the newest item, Playtex nursers, which were plastic containers with plastic envelopes for the milk. The envelopes were disposable. At that time, doctors were not pushing women to breast feed. If you were a good mother, you used disposable bottles and disposable diapers. And Terri wanted to be a very good mother.

The due date came and went. Terri had contractions often that lasted over an hour but then they would stop. Her doctor told her she was dilating slowly but the baby wasn't ready yet. Dean was a patrolman on the midnight shift so he was gone 6 nights a week. Terri was having periods of contractions that would last an hour or so but nothing had happened even though she was three weeks past her due date.

      Finally, the time came. Terri woke up about 3:00 A.M. She was surprised that she was sleeping on her stomach because she hadn't been able to do that for weeks. When she got out of bed, her water broke. She called the doctor as she had been instructed to do. Since she was not having any contractions, he told her to stay home until they were five minutes apart. She hung up the phone and had her first contraction. Five minutes later, she had another one and it continued every five minutes. Quickly, she called the Police Station to notify her husband. Dean worked from 10 P.M. to 6 A. M. on that shift. Even though Dean had told the radio room for weeks that his wife was having a baby soon. Somehow, that night a substitute operator was on duty. He didn't understand what Terri was telling him and more importantly, he didn't understand that she was three weeks past her due date. The radio room operator finally put out the call. Dean and Terri had a police scanner radio at home, and she heard the call go out. A few minutes later, she heard car tires screeching outside the house. Sure enough, Dean had driven the squad car into the yard and ran into the house. As Terri was explaining that the contractions were about three minutes apart and quite strong. Dean couldn't focus on her. He was talking to another policeman who had arrived. He was telling the other officer what to do with his police gear and his reports. He wasn't watching or listening to Terri at all. As Terri was bending over due to the severity of the contractions, Dean continued to talk because he was trying to clear his head and get his gun and gear taken care of. Finally, Terri told Dean they had to go and they had to go NOW!

Dean drove her in the police car with flashing police lights to Memorial Hospital. He wanted to use the siren but Terri talked him out of it. They finally got to the ER door. It had been a slow walk up to the door. Terri had to stop every few seconds due to the contractions. The door was locked!! It was another slow walk back to the police car. They drove around to the other door and once inside, they ran into another officer who asked what they were doing there! The other officer had just looked at Dean and thought he was bringing in a person as a result of a police call. Then he looked and recognized Terri and realized what the urgency was. Finally a nurse came out and took over and got Terri taken to the maternity floor for prepping. The hospital put Dean to work filling out insurance information.

As Terri was led into her labor room and told to change her clothes into a gown. She felt like the baby was going to drop out of her and onto the floor. But the baby didn't. Finally she was in a bed, Dean was in the room and the nurse said. "Well, I'm going to give you a little medicine to move this along, but don't push even if you feel like you have to."

She left the room and about two minutes later, Terri told Dean she felt like she had to push and could not hold it back. Dean got the nurse, she checked and said Terri was dilated to 8 centimeters. It was now about 4:30 A.M. The nurses told Terri her doctor wasn't there yet and they were going to wait for him. After a couple more strong contractions, the nurse checked and said "We can't wait, get her to the delivery room."

In those days, the fathers were not allowed in the delivery room and they didn't even put mirrors up for the mothers. Terri moved over on the table, they put another IV in her hand and the next contraction came. The on-call doctor came in, checked and said "With the next contraction, you can push a little."

Terri told him the contraction was starting. She pushed and it felt like her body was splitting in two. Then she heard a cry from the baby. The doctor told her the baby's head was out but not to push...**As if!!!** At that time, her family doctor walked in. The on- call doctor told her to wait while he checked the cord and then let her push and the baby popped out. It was 4:45 A.M. As the doctor checked her over, he told her if she was ever pregnant again, to come directly to the hospital with her first contraction because subsequent births would be come even faster.

As they worked on Terri, she got a quick look at her baby before they took him away to be checked over. She was still in the delivery room when a nurse came in to tell her that the South Bend Police Department. had just called and she had given them all the vital statistics. Terri asked what Dean had said. The nurse said, "Oh, we haven't told HIM yet!" Terri asked them to tell the new father that he had a son right away.

Then they wheeled Terri out, Dean was there and they went to the nursery to see the baby. It was a boy, 6 lbs. 8 ozs. His name was Daniel Gregg.

By the time Terri was in her room and getting settled in, it was about 6:00 A.M. Dean and Terri talked quietly about the baby and how happy they were. Terri asked Dean to call her family and his family to let them know the good news. Terri called her workplace at 8:00 A.M. to tell them she had finally delivered a baby – three weeks late. Of course, that evening several people came to visit and to see the new addition to the family.

Two days after that, they took their baby boy home. Patricia had promised to help Terri the first two weeks with the baby. But, because Terri had been late in delivering, Patricia had committed to working at the *Tribune* for someone's vacation, so Terri was on her own.

Dean had to return to work at night and sleep during the day. In addition, Dean was working a part-time job in the afternoon to make extra money. Terri learned how to be a mommy all on her own. Unfortunately Daniel had colic. **Bad…!**

Terri was home with their newborn son. She was exhausted and the baby had colic. His worst times were during the night. The doctor had given her a prescription for her son. He got two drops by an eye dropper before he had his bottle. She was supposed to wait ten minutes after he got the medication before she fed him a bottle so the prescription had time to settle his stomach.

One morning, about 3:00 A.M., Terri got out of bed when the baby started crying. She staggered into his bedroom, changed his diaper, and got the eye dropper filled. Terri put the dropper into his mouth and he inhaled at the same time. He choked! Terri panicked! Terri turned him upside down and patted his back. He didn't respond.

Terri grabbed her well-worn and well-read and often-used, hand-me-down Dr. Spock paperback book. She held her son, stomach side down with his head a little lower. In-between patting his back, she flipped through the index of the book. She couldn't get him to respond at all. He was never quiet! He should be hungry. Actually, he should be starving because it had been four hours since his last feeding. Terri found the section about choking. She took him into the bathroom, held him by his little legs with his head down, and smacked his back twice.

Nothing happened! He was limp, and did not respond to flicking the bottom of his foot with her fingernail. Terri cried, she begged him to wake up. She gently shook him a little bit but nothing happened. Terri was convinced she had killed her newborn baby. Terri felt like a terrible mother. Terri was sure she was being punished because she had wanted a baby girl. She didn't know anything about boys so she was sure that this was all her fault. Now she had no choice but to call the ambulance. The Fire Department ambulance came quickly. The two huge firemen came rushing into the house. They checked the baby over, looked at the prescription bottle, checked him again and then they said...

"All of our equipment is too large for a newborn infant of this size and weight. We think he is ok but we want to take him to the emergency room for a doctor to make sure."

Terri's husband was actually on his night off and had been sleeping throughout this whole situation. Terri didn't wake him while the drama had been unfolding because she didn't want him to know she had probably killed their child. But now he had to be told and they had to drive to the emergency room. Terri was still recovering from the birth and not getting much sleep either so her thought processes were slow.

Terri woke her husband and gave him a quick run down on what had happened. They both threw on some clothes and followed the ambulance carrying the two firemen and their newborn son. They arrived at the emergency room and waited outside for the doctor to call them in. When they were taken into the emergency room cubicle; they saw their little 6 lb 8 oz. naked baby boy on a huge stretcher. He was on his back, his eyes were closed. He wasn't moving at all. Terri thought she was going to faint. Then the doctor asked her to explain what had happened. She went through the process, crying and shaking. She was waiting for his final diagnosis on the cause of death. She expected him to accuse her of neglecting her baby boy.

He said, "When you patted the baby's back, apparently you knocked the air out of him. Then the medication took over. He fell asleep. He is sleeping so well because there is no colic in him now. He has no fluid in his lungs. He is just fine.

You did not hurt him. He is just asleep. He will probably wake up very hungry soon. Now, do YOU need something to calm you down so you can sleep?"

"OH NO!" Terri said. "I have to be awake to feed him when he wakes up." Daniel Gregg did not wake up until 8:00 A.M. the next morning. He was refreshed and ready to go. Terri was not.

He finally got over colic after a few more months and became a very easy baby to care for and a wonderful little boy to raise. That little newborn baby boy recently celebrated his 43rd birthday.

He spent a lot of his childhood with his Grandmother Patricia. He was her first grandchild. Living just a few houses away, throughout most of his childhood, afforded them time to spend together. He was also very attached to his Grandpa Ray. Daniel was allowed to play on his block with the other children. Some days, Daniel would walk down to his grandparents' house which was on the same side of the street as his house. Daniel used to knock on the door to see if Grandpa would "come out to play." If Raymond was too tired, there were still a few cookies to enjoy while Daniel talked about his busy day at school or playing with his neighborhood friends.

Terri had been in contact with her father, Donald, ever since his visit to take her out to dinner in 1963. During those years, she often filled him in with long letters about what was going on in her life. When she found out she was pregnant, she was so thrilled to tell Donald that he soon would be a grandfather to his oldest daughter's child. And when Daniel was born, Terri wrote Donald immediately to tell him everything about the new baby.

A couple of years later, Terri received a Christmas card from Donald and his wife, Dorothy. It had a printed signature. There was no handwritten message, no news, nothing personal. That really hurt Terri's feelings. She stopped writing to Donald. He didn't write her either. She just couldn't understand what had caused the estrangement. Many years would go by before they reunited.

In the early 1970's, Terri told her mother that she always had wanted to be the mother of twins. Terri had read a book in the 5th grade and fell in love with the names of the twin girls....Tricia and Tracy. She had always planned to name her twin daughters those same names. Her father, Donald, had twin brothers and

Dean's side of family had twins also. Terri was shocked when Patricia told her that she, Patricia herself, was a twin. She was even more astonished when Patricia revealed she had no idea where her father or her twin brother were. And even sadder was that Patricia had not seen her twin brother since she was a very small child. It seemed like the most depressing story that Terri had ever heard.

1980's

The next few years went by quickly. Terri and Dean had talked about have a second child but when it didn't happen as they hoped, they decided that one child was enough. Terri wanted Dean to have time with his son. She didn't want him to work a second job any more. She got a job when Daniel started first grade. She learned to drive a car….at last. They had a dog and a cat and life was going along very well. They moved to an older home in the country and a few years later, Daniel graduated from high school.

1990

By early 1990, Patricia was living alone. Her husband, Raymond, had passed away. Patricia had gone back to work when Raymond retired. She had a job as a proofreader for Ava Maria Press in South Bend. She also took some art classes at the Art Center, learning about the various types of art and the variety of artists. In return for this free education, she became a docent for the Art Center. She had an opportunity to give tours and to attend the various showings throughout the year. Additionally, she also took up a new passion... ballroom dancing. She loved it. I am sure she fantasized that she was dancing in Paris when she attended the classes. She also joined a dance group that performed for some of the senior nursing homes around the area.

She took a class in creative writing. She discovered some joy in writing stories and poetry. She worked on a newsletter for the ballroom dancing studio where she took lessons. She enjoyed writing poems featuring the various dances and made up little quizzes for the newsletter too. Some magazines and the local newspaper had contests. She often entered the contests and would use a pen name in order to try for various prizes. And she did. She often won in more than one category under more than one pen name within the same contest.

***

Blue Birthday

It's my birthday and no one remembered
No birthday cards, no ringing of the phone
No one is sending their best wishes
No one at all, indeed I'm quite alone.
But I have memories of sweeter times
When there were gifts and kisses by the score
Yes, I remember all the lovely yesterdays
And how I wish they could be mine once more.
Oh how I'd treasure every moment
When flowers bloomed and skies were blue
But here again, it is my birthday
And I'm alone and missing you.

***

CAR BLUES

I'm feeling like a princess
Or a well known TV star
As I buzz along the highway
In my brand new, shiny car.
I'm breaking in the feeling

Of a high that's unexpected
People show their warm approval
Of the color I've selected.
They discuss my car's efficiency
And the mileage I'll enjoy
I know that I'm the envy
Of every girl and boy.
Yes, it's great to be the owner
Of a car so bright and new
My only day of sorrow
Is the day a payment's due.

***

TWO WEEKS WITH PAY

Whether you go to the seashore
Or climb a mountain or two
Getting away for a brief holiday
Is bound to be good for you.
Whether you drive cross country
Or take a ship for a cruise
When you suddenly fly 'neath a soft summer sky
You're sure to lose the blues.
So pack your bag for a journey
Hurry and don't delay
You can give the slip to your troubles on a trip
Especially with two weeks with PAY.

***

TO A YOUNGER LOVE

When I look at you, I see the fact
That I am older in my years.
That I was growing and going to school
Before you'd shed your baby tears.
The things that you're discovering
Are all old hat to me
And I cannot act as youthful
As you'd often like me to be.
And so I fear one day our love
Like winter snow will melt.
And you will find another
Who'll know the love I've felt.
But remember the sweet days we've shared
When time stood still for a while
And I will keep you in my heart
And wrap my love in a smile.

***

MOTHER'S DAY AT MCDONALDS

There's a woman who comes to McDonalds
About 10 o'clock each day
And she quietly watches the children
As they gaily romp and play.
There's a tender smile that hovers
Over lips now pale and old
And she gently dreams of the past again
While her cup of coffee grows cold
She remembers her children laughing

And how quickly they were grown
How silently the years flew by
Till now she is alone.
So if you see this lady
Just nod and say "hello"
She'll appreciate your kindness
She's a mother still, you know.
***

As Patricia's life continued, she felt content. She did the things she loved. She lived alone but all of her daughters were involved in her life. Bonnie came back from California to live with Patricia for a few months. Ginny was married with two children and lived in Illinois. Mary was away at college. Terri and Dean lived in the country just minutes away. For years, Terri, Daniel, and Patricia went to the library on Saturday together. They used that time to catch up on the weekly activities each one had. Afterward, they would stop for lunch. Many times, Dean would take a lunch break from his job on the Police Department to meet them for a few minutes to talk.

Then came a day that changed everyone's life forever. Mary was home for the summer. Bonnie was visiting for the weekend. They had gone out for lunch with Terri and Daniel. Patricia had seemed a bit anxious that

day. She didn't talk very much and just seemed to be thinking of something else. Finally, she pulled out a piece of stationery and gave it to Terri. This is what it said....
***

July 12, 1990

Dear Mrs. Gregg:
 Mr. Jack J. Hill, address xxxxxxxxx, Cityxxxxxx, New York, telephone number xxxxx, would like to get in touch with you.
 Because of the circumstances, we agreed to send this letter. However, we have not revealed your address, and we will not tell Mr. Hill whether the letter is delivered. You are free to reply or not, as you choose. In any event, you need not notify us of your decision.

Sincerely,

Office of Public Inquiries
Dept of Health & Human Services
Social Security Administration.
 ***

 Jack J. Hill was Patricia's twin brother. They were 66 years of age, separated when they were about 4 years old. And now, Patricia had a chance to find out about her other

family...and.....meet her twin brother.
What would she do?

THE TWINS

Patricia was now almost forced to review her life. She had always thought that she was a fortunate woman. In spite of the difficulties growing up during the Depression, she always felt loved. In spite of learning when she graduated from high school that her life had really started in Oklahoma, she didn't feel cheated. In spite of learning that Bill was not her real father, she knew he loved her. In spite of marrying young and getting a divorce, she thought she had come through it very well. And now, in spite of the death of her second husband, Raymond and the serious illness and unexpected death of Ginny's little six year old son, she felt she had gotten through some tough times and created a new life for herself.

But now.....the reality of finally learning about her life from the time of her birth was frightening. She had tried over the years to contact her birth father and had been rudely rebuffed. She was almost afraid that the letter from Social Security might cause her even more pain. She had managed to put that part of her early life out of her mind. Did she really want to take the chance?

Should she?

Would she?

COULD SHE?

Most of the people she had trusted throughout her life were gone. Her mother, Josephine, had died in 1945, Uncle James Leonard had died in 1967. Her beloved ex-mother-in-law, Leonette, had died in 1970 of a heart attack. Her dear Aunt Lucille, who always encouraged her to try to find her birth father, had passed in 1982. Her stepfather, Bill, had died in 1982. Even her second husband who had been her loving companion for many years was gone.

She had three of her four daughters still involved in her life. Bonnie lived south of Indianapolis. Ginny did not keep in touch with her sisters or her mother often. Ginny had taken the death of her son very hard and placed her anger on other things including blaming her mother for past issues. Mary was always a source of adventure and encouraged her mother to follow her heart. Terri was married, had a son and a busy career, and saw her mother at least once a week on a regular basis for many years.

Patricia wrote this about her daughters....in 1991

"Last summer I took 3 different short vacations - each one with a different daughter and grew to know each child a bit better.

The first trip was with Bonnie and we visited Mackinaw Island for a 4 day weekend. Bonnie is the third of my four daughters and was the "baby" for eleven years before Mary; the fourth and last child was born.

Bonnie and I share an overgrown Irish imagination and love of the melodramatic. We quickly changed our persona to fit the adventures that awaited us in our travel. I became **Lilith McDowell**, a freelance travel writer and Bonnie changed her name to **Liz Devereux** on the lookout for sites to film educational movies. We indulged in these fantasies only among ourselves. We dined on white wine and shrimp salad luncheons in our public appearances and then pigged out on KFC and candy bars in the privacy of our motel room. We did the requisite touristy things on Mackinaw Island. The horse drawn carriage ride, buying

Island fudge and T-shirts, seeing the Fort and other attractions, but we also spend hours talking of men, marriage, morals and manners. Also Madonna, meals, makeup and motherhood. We came home with a new appreciation of each other that bridged the generation gap.

My second trip was a visit to New York City, a place my husband had always refused to go. He hated the traffic and noise but Mary, my fourth daughter, and I flew into LaGuardia and then took a taxi to our hotel, situated in the middle of the theater district. We quickly learned of the cut-rate ticket outlets and spent 2 hours of our first day standing in line for show tickets that went on sale for that night's performances. We bought tickets for a blues musical revue BLACK & BLUE and also for GYPSY for the following evening with Tyne Daily in the starring role. Also during our stay, we took a guided bus tour through upper New York City, Central Park, Wall Street and passed many of the imposing hotels where the rich and famous have suites. We also took a bus trip that led us through Greenwich Village and Chinatown where we had dinner. Saturday included a ferry boat trip to view the Statue of Liberty, the skyline at night ablaze with a million lights and a passing parade of every nationality on the face of the earth. The awe and reverence shone towards the Statue of Liberty was tremendous. Cameras were clicking like popcorn and excited voices in a dozen different dialects beat on my ears.

DEAR READERS....*I must interrupt this story written by Patricia to tell you what she did regarding that letter from Social Security...*
    Patricia asked her daughters, after they read the letter for themselves, what to do. She told her daughters about how she had been turned away years before with a returned letter and a rude conversation on the telephone. She was afraid. She was anxious. She was unsure. Her girls all encouraged her to call. They all were so shocked that she had not heard about or known about her twin brother for over sixty years. Now she had a chance to find out what happened and so...
    SHE CALLED! The phone was answered by a woman. Patricia prepared herself to be on receiving end of another rude conversation. She explained that she had received a letter from Social Security and before she could say another word, the woman

asked very quickly. "Are you Jack's sister?" Patricia told the woman her name and the next thing she heard was "Jack, come quickly. Your sister is on the phone!"

Patricia was so nervous that she barely remembered the conversation with Jack. All she did remember was telling him she had coincidentally already planned a trip to New York City. Jack told her he would send her a letter with directions because he lived close enough that she could take a train to his town. He was so happy to hear from her and wanted to meet her face to face as soon as possible.

July 20, 1990

Dear Patricia:

It's hard to believe we have finally made contact! I really thought it was going to happen one day but it was still a real surprise when you said you were Patricia on the phone. I had sent a letter to my New York Senator, Alfonse D'Amato, and asked if he would contact Social Security and request a name check. That was on May 29, 1990.

I'm happy to hear you were planning on coming to New York soon. You will have to plan on coming up to see us. I am enclosing a train schedule and you can see there are a number of trains each day from New York City to xxxxxx. We also have an airport in xxxxx where American Airlines, Continental, Delta, Eastern and Northwest are available. If you wish, you could fly home from xxxx.

In the last two years I've become interested in genealogy and have been able to trace the Hill family back to 1777 and the Crim family back to about 1820. I am enclosing a page on my family and also one on our ancestors.

Our two daughters both live here in the Northeast. Bonnie lives in Vermont and two hours away and Joan lives in Pa, about six hours away.

I forgot to mention it when you called. Our older brother Jimmie was killed in the war in 1943 in an Air Force training flight. He had married in 1942. I had met his wife when he and I worked in Ca. After his death there was very little contact with his wife and I don't know what happened to her.

My wife, Florie and I have lived in New York since 1948 in various locations. Florie and I are looking forward to seeing you and your daughter, Mary. We have plenty of room and would love to show you some of the upstate New York.

Love Jack and Florie
***
So to continue with Patricia's essay....
"Our last day was spent on a train from New York City speeding to xxxxx, N.Y. where I was destined to meet my twin brother for the first time in over 60 years. But that's another story. Mary's youthful sense of adventure made the overpriced and underdone meals all worth while during our trip to New York"
***

Patricia and Jack had a good first meeting. A local newspaper came to the train station, took pictures, and wrote an article about the two. Patricia and Jack were fraternal twins. Although they did not have all the same features, they did share a few. Their eyes were the same light hazel; they had several identical mannerisms and they enjoyed many of the same things including music, reading, and chocolate. Their upbringing had been very different. One was raised by his father and the other raised by her mother. Their childhood experiences and opportunities and life choices were not the same.

Jack had been married to his wife Florie for many years. He had been employed by the State of New York for over thirty years and also been retired from Union College in Schenectady for ten years. He had traveled often and had lived a comfortable and interesting adult life. He had two daughters. And oddly enough, his youngest daughter was also named Bonnie just as was Patricia's third daughter. The daughters of each twin even resembled each other. His older daughter, Joan, looked very much like Mary in her facial features and her hair color and style. And both of the Bonnies had dark eyes and short dark hair.

Jack had no recollection of his mother, Josephine. In fact, what he had been told by his stepmother, Dolly, was not very flattering or in some cases even true. He had a very real anger about Josephine. Until he talked to Patricia and she was able to tell him what their mother was really like, he had no interest in learning about her. Once Patricia shared her version of Josephine, he became much more comfortable with seeking information, photos and stories about their mother. He did tell Patricia that after their father married his second wife, Dolly, life was very harsh for the boys. He said Dolly never was affectionate. She cooked, cleaned, and cared for the home but did not enjoy her role as a stepmother. Jack is sure that it was Dolly who returned Patricia's letter years before and also was the woman who so cruelly talked to Patricia on the telephone. He did recall that Dolly told him when he was 40 years old that he had a twin sister who might be trying to contact him. His stepmother said he should have nothing to do with her. After that, Jack said he waited for a letter or another phone call to come but it never did. He also thought his father would talk about it at some time but his father never mentioned a previous marriage. He then was sure that when his father passed in 1989, he would have left a letter explaining the details, but there was no letter. Back in those days, families did not often discuss their pasts or talk about personal issues.

That was when Jack decided he would have to try to find his sister himself. And so he did. He was very happy and very surprised when his sister called a few weeks after the letter had been sent. They didn't exchange any pictures before they met for the first time but knew each other instantly and felt a connection.

In October of 1990, Jack and his wife came to South Bend to meet Patricia's daughters and families. The *Tribune* did an article about the twins' reunion, including photos and an interview with them.

Right about this same exciting time in their lives, Terri received a letter from her cousin. Her cousin had heard that Donald was ill. He had colon cancer. Terri wanted to make contact with him and got his new address. They started corresponding frequently and made plans to see each other.

A few weeks later, both Patricia and Jack were contacted by the University of Minnesota Twin Research group. They were conducting research on twins who had been separated at a very young age. They wanted to determine what traits were genetic and what was environmental. The research study offered to pay for the twins, Jack's wife Florie, and Patricia's daughter, Terri to come. They would be using Florie as an environmental research side study and Terri as a genetic blood relative to check other variables of the research study.

This brings me to the rest of Patricia essay on vacations with her daughters...

..."My third and last trip was to Minneapolis, Minn. on a week-long trip and stay at the University of Minnesota. This was a research project testing twins who had been reared apart. My twin brother, Jack and I, plus a family member, each were tested in every conceivable way. Jack brought his wife and I brought Terri, my oldest daughter as a family member and a traveling companion. Our expenses were paid by the University of Minnesota and though we put in long days of tests, from 8:00 A.M. until 5:00 P.M. for six days, most of our evenings were free. Jack and I had a lot of time to talk and catch up on each other's lives. It was an exhausting week, mentally and physically and I was glad to have Terri along. She is very efficient and reliable, plus Terri and I had a chance to talk without the others around in our motel room, and on the plane trip to and from Minneapolis.

My three trips were all different as my daughters are also different but there was pleasure and a sense of discovery in each one – both in the trips and my daughters.

***
November 16, 1990

Dear Ones:
    Should fill you in on my trip to Minneapolis and so here goes.
    We arrived about 2 P.M. Saturday and received a phone call shortly from Nancy Sxxx, Asst. to Prof. Bxxx. We'd be picked up at noon Sunday and start our mental testing. We were at the Univ. for six hours on Sunday and really had our brains picked. It was a general intelligence test and covered a little bit of everything. We also had 4 work books – each about an inch thick which contained 100s of questions to which we were to answer Yes or No....or sometimes Never, Seldom, Occasionally, Often or Always. We were told we would have answered about 15,000 questions by the time we are done.
    There were about 100 basic questions in each book but worded in various ways so you couldn't get away with a lie very often. We worked from 8 A.M. till 5 P.M. each day – but Tuesday when we stayed until 9 PM. We were sent home in blood pressure sleeves that measured our blood pressure all night long every 10 minutes. The pressure of inflation was enough to keep you awake all night.

Terri and Florie had to wear that contraption the next night. They had some of the same tests we did but not all. Terri did more than Florie as she was a blood relative. We were weighed and measured in every possible way, nose to mouth, ear to ear, shoulder to elbow, knee to ankle and etc.

We had an eye test, dental exam, manual dexterity, spelling, reading comprehension, color blindness, retention of numbers, math, I.Q. and more. Also handwriting specimens, several private interviews with an assistant on life stresses, life as a child, then Nancy did an interview with me on SEX which included my sexual fantasies. I started to concoct a story for her. I got carried away and told her an entire Gothic romance. She couldn't shut me up as I spewed forth every titillating tidbit in my imagination. Poor woman! She was as worn out as I was when I finished. Wish I could have taped it and sold it to Harlequin Romance!

Jack, Florie, Terri and I usually had breakfast and dinner together and we had some grand meals. Terri had to spend time with Florie when Jack and I were being tested but she bore up pretty well. All in all, it was an exciting and exhausting experience and I'd love to do it again.

Ok, according to Jack, we are eligible for DAR membership if you care.

Love Mom
**

Everyone enjoyed the research project but were more than glad to go back home to settle back into their own lives and see what was in store for them in the future.

DEAR READERS: Just a quick edit to the last letter. When Patricia said in a letter that "Terri bore up well" having to spend time with Aunt Florie....what she meant was that Aunt Florie had a short term memory problem. She couldn't remember what she said or was told from one minute to the next. She was constantly asking **Who was you? Why are you here? Where was Jack, her husband? Did you know Jack? How did you know Jack? Wasn't Jack handsome? Why were you here? Who are you? Who is Patricia? Did you know that Jack had a sister he had never met? Who are you? Why are you here? Where was Jack? Did you know Jack?** And on and on and on..... And yes, it was exhausting.

One day the twins had all day sessions and Florie and Terri were on their own. Jack did not want to leave

Florie alone in a strange city or even in the hotel room so Terri was asked to take her for a walk downtown, go shopping, and have lunch. When Terri realized that Florie could not remember who Terri was and was confused about the reason she was with her, Terri was very concerned about taking her out in public for fear that Florie would walk away or that she would get frightened and want Terri to leave her alone. So, Terri managed to get her out of a store. They had lunch and then they went back to the hotel. Terri stayed with her in her room until Uncle Jack and Patricia got back. Needless to say, Terri didn't want to have dinner with them that night. She wanted to order room service and have silence!!!!! Patricia understood perfectly!

After the twin study was completed, Jack and Patricia returned to their own homes. The Research project had also included physical examinations. Each of the twins was told they should have their eyes examined. Patricia was told she might have the beginning of cataracts. She did see her doctor and did have some laser surgery which corrected the problem.

The twins continued to correspond. Jack became quite interested in researching the family tree and often requested pictures from Patricia. He also shared pictures he had of their older brother and their father. Whenever he discovered something new about the family, he would let Patricia know.

LIFE CHANGES – 1992

A couple of years earlier, Mary had been married to a man she met at college in Texas. She was married in the First United Methodist Church in South Bend. It was the same church the family had attended ever since they first moved to South Bend many years before.

In 1991, Mary, Patricia's youngest daughter, was pregnant with her first child. She had moved to Connecticut with her husband. She asked Patricia to come out when the baby was born so she would have someone to talk to and someone to help her out.

The baby, Anna Elizabeth, was born on January 17, 1992. Patricia did go out but she didn't seem to have much energy. She didn't want to cook and didn't seem as interested or as excited about the new baby as Mary had expected. Since Mary was breast feeding her baby, about the only time she got any rest was when Patricia would hold the baby. Mary was doing everything else including the cooking, cleaning, laundry, grocery shopping and all. On top of that, Mary had had a Caesarian so she was especially tired and still healing.

Time passed by quickly. Patricia continued to enjoy her private life. She spent a lot of time reading and resting at home. She was involved in a line dance group with the Battell Senior Center. They put on a little dance demonstration downtown one warm summer day. After their performance, she sat down and noticed her clothes felt tight. She didn't think she had gained weight but was very surprised to see her abdomen bloating out in front of her eyes. When it didn't go away after a couple of days, she went to her family doctor. After several questions and some prodding, she admitted to her doctor that she had not been feeling well for several weeks. He discovered what seemed to be a large hernia. She was sent to a specialist and hernia surgery was set up. She came through the surgery but just didn't seem to regain her strength. She spent even more time just reading and napping at home.

A few months later, Mary planned her baby's christening. Patricia had still not regained her own strength. Terri went out for the special occasion instead of Patricia. Terri was the godmother and felt more like she was the grandmother. She was so happy to spend time with Mary and her husband and of course, the new baby girl, Anna Elizabeth.

Patricia's family doctor was also Terri's doctor. When Terri went in for a regular appointment, the doctor asked her about her mother. Terri told him that she wasn't herself; she seemed to be extremely tired and was becoming like a recluse at times. He asked Terri to urge Patricia to make another appointment.

In 1992, as a result of further testings, it was determined that Patricia was having some serious problems with her liver. She had been diagnosed with Hepatitis several years before. This was before the medical profession knew much about the disease. They thought she had eaten some tainted fish when she traveled to Canada or even Europe. Or she could have possibly been exposed to the Hepatitis as a result of surgery. She had fallen a few winters before, breaking her ankle. She had surgery to put pins in and it was possible that she was given some affected blood in a transfusion. She had never been a drinker or abused drugs so they were not certain how the Hepatitis had occurred.

Patricia was given several pills to take and continued to live by herself at home. She seemed to get better. Mary brought Anna Elizabeth for a visit and Bonnie had come back for a visit too. Patricia and her daughters and her grand daughter had a great time together.

The next time, Terri saw her doctor, he asked about Patricia's living arrangements and encouraged Terri to talk to Patricia about moving where she would have daily contact with someone. He told Terri that the disease Patricia had was terminal. Hopefully, the medication would slow down the progression of the disease but it would never go away. He also told her that Patricia was going to continue to deteriorate.

Dean and Terri had moved back into town and had a two bedroom, two bathroom townhouse. Dean and Terri had been discussing asking Patricia to move in with them for several years, especially after Raymond died. Patricia could not keep up with the maintenance on her house and really had no idea what she needed to do when a household problem came up. Now the doctor was implying that this disease was progressing and that Patricia needed to be pushed into getting more help. Terri had several conversations with Patricia in which she always said " No, I'm just fine living alone." Terri didn't want to take away her mother's independence and certainly didn't want Patricia to feel that she was so sick she couldn't make her own decisions.

Her mother had another terrible problem because the hernia came back. She didn't call Terri until two days after she had been up all night coughing up blood. Terri insisted that she go to the hospital to be checked over. Terri was asked to go back to the ER area to help her mother dress. It was the first time Terri saw the huge hernia and she nearly passed out from the shock. It was then that Terri knew that Patricia was in real trouble. She needed another surgery but her doctor said she was too weak to handle it. She was obviously losing weight. She just didn't have her usual desire to go anywhere. She had aged and gotten dramatically frail and seeing her without her usual layers of baggy clothing made it very apparent.

Terri had lunch with her mother one Saturday. She asked Patricia to come live with them again. Patricia said she didn't want to be a burden. Dean had come to have lunch with them and Terri took advantage of his strength and support. Terri told Patricia it was more of a burden to worry every time the phone rang that Patricia was hurt or had been lying on the floor because no one was there to help her. Terri told her it would be a huge relief to all of them if she would move in. She told her mother if Patricia wouldn't do for herself, would she please do it for Terri.

Daniel had graduated from high school. He had a job. He had moved out and was living on his own. So the townhouse had a large bedroom with an attached full bath on the main level that Patricia could have as her own. It was large enough for all her bedroom furniture plus a large overstuffed chair and ottoman. She would have room for her own television and have her own walk-in closet. Dean and Terri both worked full time so Patricia would be alone during the day and still have company in the evenings and on the weekends.

Patricia finally agreed to move in. Terri and Dean and Daniel started to go through all the things in Patricia's house because they would have to sell it. Patricia was asked to pick a paint color for her new bedroom at the townhouse so they could paint before she moved in. They made all the arrangements to move her personal belongings that she would need. Terri ordered address labels for Patricia as a surprise so she could write to all her relatives about her new home.

As of March, 1993, Patricia was now a member of the household. They were all settling in and things seemed to be going well. Patricia admitted within days that she was very happy in her new home and loved it. She said she would never regret moving in and felt so safe and secure there.

Dean, Terri, and Daniel continued to clear out Patricia's house. There was very little of value except for personal items. They gave away a lot of the old furniture. By an odd quirk of fate, a few days later, a storm came through and a tree fell through the roof. Terri would not take Patricia to see the damage because she knew it would upset her. Terri made arrangements with the insurance company. The house was repaired and repainted. The repairs actually brought the house more up to date. The house was put up for sale and a few weeks after that, a realtor called. The realtor had discovered the bathroom toilet leaked and all the floors and carpet were damaged. Another claim was filed and again the house was repaired. By replacing the old carpet with a nice new current color, replacing the old linoleum tile with a more modern press-on tile color, repainting the walls, and replacing the old metal kitchen cabinets, that had been damaged by the roof caving, in with wood shelves, the house actually looked better than it ever had before. Raymond had considered himself the "do-it-yourself" man and had rigged up some varied little projects over the years that actually did nothing for the house. The little projects gave him something to do, Patricia didn't really care what it looked like. It had worked for them. But now, in order for the house to be appealing to a buyer, the fresh repairs made a huge difference in the possibility of selling it.

Since the tree came through the roof and the toilet leaked, it allowed Terri to get the old decor torn out, get some cleanup done which, in turn, saved the insurance company money and made the house look much more modern and presentable. It wasn't too long after the repairs were complete that the house was sold.

The hardest part was the day of the closing. Terri went through the house to say "goodbye." It made her feel so sad to think that her mother never got to live in the house after the repairs were done. It looked so much better than it ever had before. Patricia never asked to see the house and so Terri didn't take any pictures for her. Patricia still lived in the past and wanted to remember the home she had left instead of seeing the house as it would have been if she were still able to live on her own.

Patricia was not getting better. There were days when Patricia was very alert and days when she was so confused. Terri could always tell if it was a good day because Patricia loved to watch *Jeopardy* and *Wheel Of Fortune*. If she couldn't answer the questions quickly, Terri knew it was a bad day. She became confused about little things. She couldn't remember how to work the microwave. She forgot how to turn on the gas burner on the stove. She spilled food all over the house. Then she would not eat because she was afraid she would get sick and vomit. She was losing weight and becoming more frail looking. Even though Terri put all of Patricia's pills out for her to take, she often would not take them. Terri was never sure if Patricia swallowed the pills or if she just put them back in the pill bottles.

Patricia would try to walk around the block every day to get some fresh air. A neighbor, who lived in the townhouse attached to Dean and Terri's home, stopped Terri one afternoon to tell her that Patricia had tried to walk around their end of the block and got so tired and confused, she sat on a bench in the neighbor's garden to rest. Sharon had been a nurse and recognized Patricia's confusion and her exhaustion so she sat with her until Patricia was able to walk back into the house. Sharon said she would keep her eye out for Patricia when she was home. Sharon had a big flower garden and Patricia enjoyed sitting on the bench and admiring the flowers. She may have thought she had walked to a park setting as she talked about the flowers in the park often when Terri asked about her day.

Terri continued to have conversations with the family doctor. He was extremely supportive and told her he would do everything he could to help ease Patricia through this process.

During the week of July 4th, 1993, Mary came from Connecticut with her husband and Anna for a visit. Bonnie drove up from south of Indianapolis for a few days and everyone had a lovely time together. Bonnie returned home that weekend to go back to work. Mary and her little family planned to stay until Monday.

On the last afternoon, Mary and her husband were going to drive up to Chicago for the day. Anna was asleep in the basement family room and Terri was on vacation at home. Patricia had walked out of her bedroom to see Mary and her husband. Right after they walked out of the door and drove away, Patricia collapsed on the couch. She told Terri she needed to go to the hospital. She said she was in extreme pain and she didn't think she could walk any more.

Terri was absolutely frantic and so upset. Why did Patricia let Mary and her husband leave if she knew she had to go to the hospital? What was Terri going to do with Anna? All she could think of was how was she going to get her mother into the car to go to the ER? As she was trying to back the car up into the garage at an angle to make the walk from the kitchen to the car shorter, her neighbor drove up.

It must have been a gift from God. Terri quickly told Bruce she needed help. She explained the situation. He got Sharon (who just happened to be off work that day). Sharon said she would stay in the house so when Anna woke up and if Mary and her husband called, she could explain. (This was before cell phones so there was no way to get in touch with Mary). Bruce somehow managed to pick Patricia up in his arms and carried her to the car where Terri was waiting to drive her to the ER. It was like a well-oiled machine the way it all fell into place.

When she got to the hospital, an orderly got Patricia out of the car and took her inside. Terri was filling out the paperwork. After a brief exam and a phone call to the family doctor, Terri was told that Patricia would be admitted. Terri called her husband to tell him what had happened and went home where she thanked Sharon for staying. Shortly after that, Mary and her husband arrived back from Chicago and were advised on what had happened.

Mary and her family had to return home the next day. Patricia was stabilized in the hospital. Bonnie had received a phone call to bring her up to date. Things had calmed down once again. The doctor told Terri he was monitoring Patricia's progress.

But.....how long would that last?

Mary and her husband brought Anna Elizabeth to the hospital to visit Patricia before they started the drive back home. Anna was just beginning to talk and they coaxed her to sing the Barney song, "I love you, you love me. We're a happy family." Patricia responded to that sweet message and then settled into another nap.

Terri went to work that week. Every afternoon on her way home, she would stop at the hospital to visit Patricia. The nurses kept saying how well she was doing but Terri didn't believe them. Patricia just wasn't herself. She was very tired and didn't really seem to have the strength to carry on a conversation. Terri asked her if she wanted to talk about anything important that might be on her mind but Patricia had no special messages or thoughts to pass on and was simply happy to have Terri talk about her day at work. She did ask about her grandson, Daniel, and wanted him to stop by. Terri promised to talk to him about a visit. As the week went on, Terri felt that Patricia was losing her spirit; she was just becoming a shell of the woman she used to be. Terri talked to the doctor who agreed that the end was coming. And it was coming quickly now.

Daniel did make a trip to visit his grandmother and had a very brief visit with her. As he was leaving, Patricia called out to him that she loved him as he left the room.

During that week, Terri decided it was time to contact her sisters and let them know how serious the situation had become. She wanted her sisters to have time to decide if they wanted to come back to see their mother again. As Terri tried to tell them what was happened, she started to cry. Her son, Daniel, was there and he took the phone and gave them all the details they needed to know.

Mary lived in Connecticut. Mary quickly made arrangements for some of her friends to take care of Anna during the day and she started driving back to Indiana. Bonnie planned to drive up from the Indianapolis area as well.

On Friday afternoon, there was a knock on the door. When Terri opened the door, she saw two people she didn't expect to see. Uncle Mike and Uncle Tom, Patricia's two brothers! Uncle Tom was visiting from California. He had gone to visit his brother, Mike, who lived in Illinois. Impulsively, they decided to drive to visit their sister, Patricia. Terri quickly filled them in on what was happening. And of course, they wanted to see their sister as soon as possible. Terri took them back to the hospital. She went to see how Patricia was doing, woke her from a nap and told her there was a surprise waiting for her outside her door. She brought in the two brothers and Patricia spoke for the first time in a few days.

"What are you two boys doing here?" she asked. They responded, "Well, Patty Jean, we wanted to see you but what are you doing in the hospital?"

Terri excused herself from the room and let the three have a visit. It wasn't long before the men came out. They were shaken by the sight of their big sister being so fragile and so weak. They couldn't get over what had happened to her. They decided to spend the evening with Terri to talk about the past few years. The next day the brothers were on their way back to Illinois. They were going to contact their only other living sibling, Kathleen, to let her know about the situation. Kathleen lived in Oklahoma.

On Saturday, Terri went for another visit. She was going to talk to the family doctor after his visit with her mother. He asked if Patricia had a DNR or living will. Terri was not aware of either and he suggested that Terri try to get Patricia to make a decision and sign the proper documents.

When Patricia had moved in with Terri in March, she had asked Terri for advice. She wanted to redo her will since it had not been changed since Raymond's death. She had, at one time, considered leaving her house to Bonnie or Mary. Instead, the house had been sold when Patricia moved in with Terri and her family. So now, its ownership was not in question. By now, Bonnie was on her own, had a job and was doing well. She was divorced and maintained a friendship with her ex-husband. She was living south of Indianapolis. Patricia felt comfortable that Mary was secure with her own family in Connecticut. Terri had been married for a number of years, had a good job and a strong marriage. Patricia was also aware that her daughter, Ginny, wanted nothing to do with her and wondered if she should exclude her as one of the beneficiaries. She didn't believe that Ginny would want to have anything to do with her estate.

Terri suggested she discuss her ideas with an attorney but Terri thought it would be better to specifically name each of her daughters in the will and leave each one something. It would keep any question of Patricia being confused or causing anyone to question or to contest the will. Patricia did keep the appointment and told Terri there was a copy of the will in her room. Terri did not ask what Patricia had decided to do about the beneficiaries. Terri, Mary, and Bonnie didn't believe that Patricia had much of anything to leave anyone. All of the three daughters had often bought food and other items for Patricia when they visited. They only wanted Patricia to be safe, secure, and comfortable during her final years. Whatever Patricia might have to leave to her daughters would be happily accepted but not expected.

So, knowing that Patricia had a will but not a Living Will or a Do Not Resuscitate Order, Terri asked for the forms at the nursing station. She was told that a representative of the hospital Social Services would be a witness when she talked to her mother. She entered Patricia's room and woke her from another nap. She explained very carefully what the forms were for and asked Patricia what she wanted to do. She went over all the details and choices a second time to be certain that Patricia understood the choices she was making. After receiving a nod from the Social Services representative, Terri asked Patricia if she was ready to sign the form, again reminding her of what she was signing. Patricia apologized for her shaky signature but was responsive to the questions and signed.

Terri took the forms back to the nursing station. There, she was shocked and upset to be told that they had given her the wrong forms and Patricia had signed a Resuscitation Order. The Social Services representative told the nurse that was not what Patricia had wanted and asked for the proper form. The Social Services representative also took the improper forms back and tore them up. Now Terri had to wake her mother up again and try to get another signature. Terri was worried that her mother could not understand and would get upset. They went back into the room and awakened Patricia again. She was very confused but she made a very shaky signature on the paper. Terri asked the Social Services representative if that was going to be valid. The representative assured her that she was present when Patricia was still lucid. It was very clear that Patricia did not want any resuscitation procedures and the representative then signed as a witness.

Mary and Bonnie arrived late Saturday evening and they were both exhausted. Terri decided she would go into work on Sunday, go through all her claim files and make notes and write out instructions because she intended to go with her sisters on Monday to visit. She didn't want her sisters to be alone when they visited Patricia. She knew they would have a shock at the deterioration that Patricia had gone through in just a few days' time. Terri gave them a quick update and suggested they go visit with Patricia on Monday while she might still be able to respond.

Bonnie did not want to see her mother in that condition and would rely on Mary and Terri to keep her advised. She preferred to remember her mother as she was before, happy, cheerful, interested in life and in her daughters. By this time, Terri was emotionally exhausted. She felt she had to hold it all together for the sake of her sisters. She told her sisters what had happened and they were thankful that the Do Not Resuscitate order had been signed.

On Sunday, Terri went into her office at 8:00 A.M. She took a sandwich and a can of diet pop and worked until after 4:00 P.M. It was quiet and there were no telephones or interruptions. She was able to work through every single claim file she had. There must have been at least three file drawers full. She wrote up instruction sheets for all the payments and ordered all the reports she needed. She also wrote memos on every file so anyone could pick up the file and find a synopsis of the claim and handle it for a few days. She also left a memo on the manager's desk, on the head secretary's desk, and on the bulletin board that she had worked all day on Sunday and that she would not be in on Monday due to her mother's terminal illness. Then, she left the office.

On the way home, she stopped at the hospital. When she walked into the room, she had another shock. Her mother was lying there....looking as though she was a small child. Her body was shrunken. Her face was like a mask. She was making some small noises, but she did not appear responsive. Terri felt like she was looking at a shell...her mother's essence was not there anymore. Patricia Jean was gone in every sense of the word.

A nurse came in to check her vital signs and Terri asked if

Patricia was in pain. The nurse said the family doctor was making sure that the morphine drip was enough that she was not suffering. Terri felt it was time to have a final conversation with her mother. She took her hand and talked to her. She told Patricia it was time for her to let go. She knew that Patricia was very tired and probably wanted to see her loved ones who had passed. She told her that they were waiting for her to arrive. She told her she could dance and sing with her mother, Josephine, and her husband, Raymond. She reminded her that her sister Bettie and brother Billy were there waiting for her to read them another story and take them to the park. She said she could read her dear little grandson a bedtime story and hold him in her arms. She told Patricia she was only asking her to do one more thing. When Patricia got to heaven, Terri wanted her to find a nice girl for Terri's son, Daniel. She asked Patricia to find one that would make him a wonderful wife and give him a family. She told her she would always love her and that all of them would miss her but it was time for her to go.

Somehow she managed to say all of that without breaking into tears. She put her mother's hand back on the bed.

She looked up. The nurse was standing there with tears running down her face. The nurse said to Terri..."I don't know how you managed to do that. It was so beautiful and I am sure your mother heard every word."

Somehow Terri drove home and walked into her living room. Her son, Daniel, was there and her sisters. Terri told them what she had just done and burst into tears. Daniel immediately hugged his mother and comforted her. He told her she had done a wonderful job. Mary and Bonnie were in tears too, of course.

After a few moments, Mary said she was going to the hospital to see her mother and said if anyone wanted to go with her, it was fine. No one did so Mary made her final visit alone.

When she returned much later, she told them that she had the feeling when she went into the room that her mother was like a child. Mary said she felt like she, herself, had turned into the mother. Maybe, because she did have a young child herself, she immediately cuddled her mother's body and sang her some lullabies. She talked to her as if she were her own baby girl and whispered and kissed her before she left. She said she felt like her mother had gotten some comfort from it because she didn't make many sounds and seemed to relax as Mary held her.

THE FINALE

From about 1989 through 1993, Patricia had embraced her poetic nature and began writing poems. She had always written little limericks for some of her coworkers and she started to write some poems for her ballroom dance newsletter. She also entered some local contests with the newspaper. Since there were usually restrictions on the number of poems you could send in, Patricia used pen names. A few times, she won in different categories under the various pen names, in the same contest.

***

CHRISTMAS WALTZ

Music is playing and couples are swaying
In a Christmas Waltz.
You're here tonight and I'm filled with delight
As we Christmas Waltz.
Snowflakes are falling and my heart's recalling
The joys that we once knew.
At this time of year when I'm with you, dear
I admit it's always been true.
Won't you promise me this as our lips softly kiss
In a Christmas Waltz.

I promise my heart and that we'll never part
As the years go by.
And we'll dance once again to the lovely refrain
Of our Christmas Waltz.
  ***

LUCK OF THE IRISH

They say if you should chance upon
A busy, hardworking leprechaun
Your wishes three are his command
And he'll heap gold in your waiting hand
He'll shower you with health and joy
Enough for any man or boy
And ask that you obey his law
And not tell people what you saw
And tell them NOT where he was found
For if you do, then he'll be bound
To take away your treasure trove
And once more he'll be on the move
Until one day, some other eyes
Will chance on him with glad surprise
And he'll enrich their lives as well
If only they promise not to tell.
  ***

Easter Lilies

Easter lilies, tall, pristine
In regal splendor so serene
Calm our spirits as we pray
The Lord God be with us today.
Keep your vigil, bright and true
As we find our peace in you.
Bless the heart of everyone
And dispel the thoughts that block the sun.

Written by Kiki Von Vietinghoff*
　　***

DEATH AND TAXES

Death and taxes
Two things we can't ignore;
And when old April rolls around
We have to pay once more.
Death and taxes
The inescapable two;
I'm glad I'll be around to pay
The second that it's due.
For if we ever had a choice
Between money and our death,
I'm sure we'd choose to live and pay
Until our final breath.
Death and taxes
Two things of which we're certain
And we'll pay an annual income tax
Until our final curtain.

Written by P. J. Hill*
　　***

AN AFTERNOON IN JUNE

The church was overflowing
And the organ would soon begin,
There was laughter among our many guests
And the assembled kith and kin.
Your mother was happily sobbing,
In her place of-honor pew
Then came the handsome groomsmen
Escorting bridesmaids dressed in blue
And soon I saw your lovely face
Your proud father at your side
My dream, my future approached me
My sweetheart, you...my bride.
Many years ago, but I remember
Our wedding and honeymoon
And never have I had cause to regret
That afternoon in June.

***

CURE FOR THE BLUES

When dining out, I'm inclined to look
For things I'd never want to cook.
Like turkey roast and golden yams
Or succulent clove-studded ham.
My desserts are creamy, mouthwatering pies
With whipped cream filled up to the skies
And chocolate cake, fit for a king
Or any calorie laden thing.
But my kitchen duties are swift and sweet
A mountainous salad, a bit of meat
But when I go out to dine

It's a 7 course dinner, replete with wine.
So when I'm sad or have the blues
I go to a restaurant and start to choose
Pizza supreme my favorite food
It's guaranteed to brighten my mood.
When you get depressed and out of sorts
Go to a place that serves course after course
Follow my lead, come on and try it
Dine in a restaurant and forget your diet.
***

THOUGHTS

The children have come home
Dragging their suitcases and their broken dreams
Behind them in a careless pile.
"Oh, what's the use", they loudly rant
And hope that I can put it all to rights
As easily as picking up a fallen tower of blocks.
But when's my time?
When I can lock the door on others' needs and wants
And spend my days and nights in sweet pursuits
Of my own pleasures and delights.
***

A QUESTION

People say there is nothing like a day at the zoo
To gaze at the animals and have them stare back at you.
Camels question you silently with a grave solemn face
As though they are asking "why are you in this place?"
Apes placidly go on with their eating or rest
And smugly convey that their life is the best.
No high level meetings, no desire to compete
Just pass the day peacefully till it's again time to eat.
So when hung up in traffic or the victim of strife,
Just ask yourself sadly...
Who's really got the best life?
* * *

NURSE AND PATIENCE

When #302 rings again
Demanding another pill.
You sympathize and realize
The woman is feeling ill.
Perhaps #304 declared each day
How awful is her diet.
You pat her head, whether blonde, brunette or red
And coax "Come on, Hon just try it"

When #327 messes her sheet
In the middle of the night
You shrug, "Oh well, what the hell
It's really quite all right."
Yes, a nurse's life is a tough one
Sometimes it couldn't be worse
Except once in a while, you get a smile
And hear a whispered, "Thank you, nurse".
***

BLESS YOU

Bless those who enter sick and ill
Bless everyone who helps to heal
The aides who answer every bell
And ask us how we really feel.
Bless ward clerks, volunteers and all
Doctors and dieticians
Interns, orderlies, student nurses
And skilled x-ray technicians.
Bless you who are always at our side
When pain must be endured
And bless the families, who welcome us home
When we are finally cured.
***

DEAR READERS: *You will note some of the poems have a different name. They were Patricia's pen names that she used to enter the poems into contests. And she won several contests too with multiple entries in the same contest.*

July 13, 1993

The telephone rang in the darkness of the early morning. Terri's husband answered and after a few words, hung up. He told Terri that Patricia had passed on. He was going to the hospital to officially identify her body, sign the release papers for the funeral home to prepare her for the funeral, and to retrieve the few personal items she had left at the hospital. Terri went to her sisters, waking them, to pass on the news. They all were in shock but relieved that Patricia's terminal illness was finally over and she was at peace.

After Dean returned home, he asked what plans they had for the day. Terri was going to the funeral home to make the final arrangements and invited her sisters to go along. She wanted them to feel part of the process even though she was the Executrix for her mother. She would also order flowers and get the announcement in the newspaper. They also discussed trying to contact Ginny, their sister. Ginny had withdrawn from the family a few years earlier. She did not answer any letters or cards and did not appear to be interested in keeping in touch with her mother or her sisters. But this was the death of her mother and all the sisters felt Ginny should have the choice of attending the funeral or not.

Dean suggested they call Ginny's husband's office. He was a doctor in the Chicago area. Terri did not have a home phone number and was not even certain where Ginny and her husband lived. A secretary at the office agreed to call Ginny at her home phone number to contact Terri. Within an hour, Ginny called Terri's home asking what was wrong. She said she would like to come back for the funeral. She got a flight for the next day. All three of the other sisters met her at the airport. She agreed to stay with all of them at Terri's home.

It was good to have all four together again even though the reason was so difficult to accept. There was some awkwardness because Ginny had chosen to withdraw from the family for several years. The other three wanted to break down the barriers in the hope that Ginny would become part of their lives again. Terri drove her by the old family house and they even visited a restaurant that they used to enjoy. They talked about their childhood and shared many memories.

Mary and Bonnie insisted that Ginny have Patricia's former bedroom for privacy. They slept on the living room floor. The three sisters were doing everything they could to make Ginny feel welcome and part of the family.

Mary's husband flew in with their daughter, Anna. Uncle Tom, Uncle Mike and his wife and Aunt Kathleen came into town along with Patricia's twin brother, Jack, and his wife Florie. There were only a few relatives left from Patricia's family. There were many friends from Patricia's former jobs, her church, the ballroom dancing group, and the Battell Center ladies along with some neighbors.

Terri suggested taking several photos and the poems that Patricia had written in the past years to the funeral home to give people something to look at and enjoy. Two of the poems were printed out for people to take as mementos. There was a huge crowd of varied people who had been in Patricia's life. The pictures and poems were well-received. There were even yellow roses with a card signed..."from a secret admirer." Yellow roses had been Patricia's favorite flower.

At the funeral, Terri asked the minister to read two poems. *Oatmeal and Kisses* was the most special and seemed to touch many hearts.

***

OATMEAL AND KISSES

Oatmeal and kisses mean Mother to me
Both were a part of my childhood, you see.
Each morning at breakfast, there would be a big bowl
And Mother would say "Eat it −it'll keep out the cold."
Whenever the family was sick or got hurt
She'd kiss away the soreness and wash away the dirt.
Her kisses were tender and sweet on my face.
And I'd lovingly hug her as we shared an embrace.
Oatmeal and kisses the best part of my youth.
The best kind of medicine and that's God's sure enough truth.
Oh how I'd love to go backward in time
And share oatmeal and kisses with that mother of mine.
But she's up in heaven probably passing a bowl
And telling an angel, "It's good for your soul."

***

The second poem was TRUE LOVE.

TRUE LOVE

You never bought me a castle in Spain
You never took me walking in the rain
But I still know our love is true
For you love me and I love you.
You never said you'd die for me
Sometimes you'd even lie to me
But when you whisper "I love you"
I'd know our love was deep and true.
So what if life's not milk and honey
And many times we're out of money
We're still together – just we two
Because our love is deep and true.
Soft lights and music don't bring love
It comes from Someone up above
And I'll thank the Lord eternally
That I've got you and you've got me.

Written by Patricia Gregg
***

Patricia passed away on July 12, 1993......69 years and 6 months and one day from the day she was born. Although she never got to meet her birth father and her older brother again before she died, she did get reunited with her twin brother and they had nearly three years to get reacquainted.

***
JULY 15, 1993...

The sisters were in the limo, riding out to the cemetery. They were talking about their mother and started laughing about some of the memories they shared. Then, Terri said "We ought to be ashamed of ourselves, our mother has recently died and we're laughing and making jokes. The funeral limo driver must think we're terrible!"

Terri's son, Daniel, was sitting in front next to the driver. He turned and said "You know, Grandma would think this was great and she would have loved it. In fact, you ought to write a book about her life but she would want you to use your real names."

And *so Terri did write that book.*
***

They were all sitting in the new, freshly waxed, very luxurious black limo thinking to themselves.

Then Terri spoke, " Damn, I just broke another fingernail."

And then Ginny said. "Well, I can see I will have to get a better manicure when I get home. There certainly aren't any good or experienced or even licensed nail shops here."

Bonnie thought, "Boy, if nothing else goes right, at least my nails always look great."

And Mary said softly, "I wish I could let my nails grow but they just get in the way when I am working."

And In addition...

On July 28, 1993 (15 days after Patricia has passed away) Donald, her first husband and father to her three oldest daughters, died. It was one week before his 70th birthday. He and Terri had renewed their relationship and spent many visits together as he battled through various types of cancer. Terri became quite close to his wife, Dorothy as well.

Terri, Bonnie, and Mary have remained very close and communicate via email several times a month. They try to spend a week or so together every July in Texas where two of the sisters live.

Ginny kept up her relationship with her sisters for a brief period of time after the death of their mother. She then sent Terri a very long detailed letter blaming Terri for everything that ever went wrong in Ginny's life.....She couldn't understand why Terri chose to be involved with their mother for so many years. She also didn't believe that Terri could love her sister, Ginny, because Terri had a relationship with their mother when Ginny did not. Terri has tried to keep in touch with Ginny during the past eighteen years. Occasionally, there is some communication. Sadly, they live about 90 miles apart but Ginny does not participate in any efforts at keeping in touch or visiting.

The story of Ginny's unhappiness would make another book and is one that only she has the right to put on paper. Her version of their childhood is sure to be much different than the other three sisters.

Terri believes that sometimes being the oldest sister means you are responsible for your siblings but does not mean that taking the blame for everything that goes wrong in a sibling's life is required by that responsibility.

And so life goes on.....

* * *

Patricia Jean Hill Drain Vietinghoff Gregg was a proofreader for the South Bend Tribune, a docent for the South Bend Regional Museum of Art, a poet, a ballroom dancer and a mother of four daughters, all of who learned to cook and clean and raise children.

Many years have passed since Patricia's death; life had changed for all of Patricia's daughters.

Terri and Dean are still married. Dean completed his twenty-year career as a police officer. Dean retired in 2008 from another job within the city government. Terri retired in 2006 after completing twenty five years as an insurance claims adjuster. She had started as a secretary and retired as a senior claims representative with a large insurance company. After her twenty five year career; she worked another five years as a customer service insurance representative for a local insurance agency.

They had one child, a son they named Daniel Gregg. In 2011, they celebrated forty six years of marriage.

Terri completed her plan to write a story about her ancestors after working over 5 years on the manuscript. Terri Jeanne Tinkel is now working on a new manuscript to be entitled **THE WHISPER** which will be loosely based on an event that occurred after her mother's death.

Their son is also married. Daniel's wife is like a daughter to Dean and Terri and they couldn't have picked a better daughter-in-law. Dean and Terri have two step grand daughters. They also have a step great grandson who was born in 2008, and a step great granddaughter who was born in 2009. The story of how Daniel and his wife first met, formed a relationship, broke up for several years, got back together and finally got married could be a book in itself.

After graduation from college, Ginny taught elementary school for a couple of years in her hometown. She married a man who was a teacher. He then went to medical school and became a doctor of internal medicine. They adopted a daughter and had a son. Their son died early in life due to cancer. Currently, Ginny is not communicating with her sisters. She lives a quiet life in Chicago with her husband. The other three sisters still have hope for reconciliation some day.

Bonnie left school early in her life. She moved around the country, got married, had three daughters and got divorced. She remarried in 1988 and got another divorce in 2000. She then remarried her second husband in

2003. They got their second divorce a few years later. She currently lives alone in Texas, where she works with the Humane Society. She stays in touch with her three daughters and with her second ex-husband.

Mary went to college, married, got her Master's degree in mathematics, moved from Texas to Kansas to Ohio to Connecticut, had two children, and taught in various states and in various school systems.

Finally, she got a job teaching in middle school in Texas, got a divorce and is currently living with her children in Texas. She teaches ESL (English as a Second Language) students in middle school.

AS A FINAL THOUGHT...

Through all the many years, the female ancestors in my family seemed to search for love and happiness. They traveled between different states in the USA. They were strong and stubborn. They loved their families. They searched for the right man to love. ***And they always kept their secrets to themselves.***

After my mother moved into my home, I made sure to bring a huge box of her journals because she wanted to keep writing. I was so anxious to read those journals after her death. But, much to my disappointment, she didn't talk about anything from her heart. She didn't explain her feelings, her choices, her struggles, her wishes or her worries. She talked about the weather, what she ate for dinner, and what she wore for a ballroom dance class. She never wrote a poem for any of her daughters or grandchildren either.

I often wonder what insights might have been gained by all four of her daughters if she had just expressed her personal thoughts in writing since she didn't speak about her past.
EVER.

Currently there are eight direct female descendants from this long line of women who are living their own lives, trying to figure it out so they can pass on their female intuition to their children and grandchildren. I hope they will share their wisdom with their female children while they can.

Terri Jeanne Tinkel
2011

Made in the USA
Lexington, KY
20 June 2015